T0149699

The Red CHAIR

When traditional psychiatry is not enough,
a psychiatrist and his patient discover
the power of past-life regression.

Dr John Webber

BALBOA.PRESS

A DIVISION OF HAY HOUSE

Balboa Press books may be ordered through booksellers or by contacting:

Balboa Press
A Division of Hay House
1663 Liberty Drive
Bloomington, IN 47403
www.balboapress.com.au
1 (877) 407-4847

Because of the dynamic nature of the Internet, any web addresses or links contained in this book may have changed since publication and may no longer be valid. The views expressed in this work are solely those of the author and do not necessarily reflect the views of the publisher, and the publisher hereby disclaims any responsibility for them.

The author of this book does not dispense medical advice or prescribe the use of any technique as a form of treatment for physical, emotional, or medical problems without the advice of a physician, either directly or indirectly. The intent of the author is only to offer information of a general nature to help you in your quest for emotional and spiritual well-being. In the event you use any of the information in this book for yourself, which is your constitutional right, the author and the publisher assume no responsibility for your actions.

Any people depicted in stock imagery provided by Getty Images are models, and such images are being used for illustrative purposes only. Certain stock imagery © Getty Images.

Cover design: Jess Webber

Print information available on the last page.

ISBN: 978-1-5043-2006-1 (sc)
ISBN: 978-1-5043-2007-8 (e)

Balboa Press rev. date: 12/09/2019

For Judy, whose courage and humour has taught me so much,
and whose spirit will go infinitely beyond this life.

Contents

Note to the reader

Psychiatrist–patient confidentiality remains an important principle in the practice of psychiatry. All the patients mentioned in this book have authorised me to write their histories. Only names, places, and other identifying details have been changed to protect their privacy. Their stories are true and unchanged.

While treating Judy, I always took detailed notes. The dialogue and interactions are therefore a close representation of our consultations.

Nearly all the past-life regressions were recorded, and unless otherwise stated, the excerpts are taken from those recordings.

Introduction

Everyone has a book in them, the saying goes, but I never thought I did. Despite having some very interesting and colourful patients like Judy, the other protagonist of this book, it remained unlikely that I would become an author.

In my thirty-six years in psychiatry, I have always used contemporary, evidence-based treatments and still do. It's well known that with these therapies, a percentage of patients does very well, the majority does pretty well, and a percentage does poorly. Judy fitted squarely into that group that has a poor response. Psychiatry's science and methods are far from perfect, a reality that I had previously been obliged to accept. Despite that, I loved working as a psychiatrist and still do.

So, what do you do when modern medicine isn't enough? It was eight years ago that I was exposed to the evidence supporting reincarnation, life after death, and consciousness existing beyond our bodies. This is the story of events surrounding that discovery. It includes the initial years of trying to treat Judy with traditional methods interrupted by my exposure to the wonderful psychic and mystical experiences of my patients and others. The narrative then leads to my introduction of hypnosis and past-life regressions with some of my patients. Eventually, that included Judy, for whom the impact was extraordinary.

Judy's life was a stark contrast to my own. For the curious, here is an abridged version of my life before meeting her. I grew up in Melbourne as one of five children, and played in neighbourhoods that were safe and friendly. I attended local schools and then, as the family finances improved, a private secondary school. Mum and Dad were raised through the Great Depression and the Second World War, and were parents of their generation: kind and loving, but not particularly demonstrative. If I ever mentioned that I thought I'd done well in an exam, Mum would remind me not to blow my own trumpet. It was clear that we were expected to behave well at home and even more so in public. As a slightly anxious child, I was a sponge for those expectations. In response, I remained driven, competitive, and ever eager to do the right thing, while also fearful of failing in the eyes of authority or the establishment—another reason why I would never contemplate writing a book, especially not one like this.

Some aspects of my childhood were memorable. Dad knew a lot of local farmers through his job, and while holidaying on a farm, if we wanted to, he would let us watch him slaughter one of the sheep. After skinning the animal, he would open the carcass and show us the gall bladder and bile and how that went to the intestines. You had to remove the gall bladder in one piece, otherwise its bitter contents contaminated everything else, and there would be none of Mum's lamb's fry or tripe for tea. Then he would reveal the heart and how it pumped blood throughout the body. The heart, not to be wasted, would become dinner for our cat Tippy. Dad would extract the lungs all in one piece and blow into what he called the windpipe while I watched in amazement as the lungs expanded. I have no doubt these experiences were important to my desire to pursue medicine as a career.

I was always strong academically, and good at sport. My final-year school results were so outstanding they made my mother gasp, and were well above the level required for entry into Melbourne University's medical school. I was blessed to attend during what I call the golden age in Australia, when university was free. It was also where I met my future wife, Kate. I was lucky indeed.

During my initial years as an intern at the Royal Melbourne Hospital, I chose surgical rotations but quickly became disillusioned. I barely got to speak to patients, and standing in theatre with a mask over my often blocked and sometimes running nose for hours on end was uncomfortable to say the least. Handkerchiefs were a big part of my childhood and remain a ubiquitous part of my daily life.

In psychiatry, I loved the combination of science and humanity. It satisfied me, so that's where I stayed. After thirteen years of university and hospitals, and having passed the specialist exams of the Royal Australian and New Zealand College of Psychiatrists (RANZCP), I was qualified as a psychiatrist and moved into private practice. By the time I met my patient Judy, I was married with four children, Kate was taking the load at home, and I was working hard as well.

I was attached to and yet limited by the ever-developing science of psychiatry, and that remained the case until I was finally and irresistibly drawn to a new view of our world. My engagement with that knowledge led to amazing insights regarding past lives, the spirit world, how we choose our lives, our connectedness to each other, and a very new perspective on who we really are. Ultimately, I was inspired to tell the story, but it was Judy who initially encouraged me to write about the events that have changed our lives.

So here's the book I was never going to write.

Judy's story

1. Mad as hell

"France … it's war. I'm French … a grey, button-up coat—it's cold—full-length, shoes, gloves, walking along a river and helping people. I'm hiding the French people and helping people. I've got a house … they're scared. … I'm male … it's my home. The people … I think they're French. I have a skinny house. You can get under the house. That's where they hide. I can hear the fighting nearby, shots and bombs.

"I'm nineteen … I'm Anoir, and I'm married. Three boys. I'm proud. Twins aged four and a little one … the kids are playing upstairs. We are hiding only three people. The soldiers are knocking on the door. The children are quiet. They would kill us all…

"The men we were hiding have left and the Germans are looking downstairs but they've gone. We are all safe, they are safe, but the Germans hit you. Their presence scares me … hit me with the gun in the face but it's alright … they got away. They're all safe…

"They've shot me. I'm twenty-two. I'm rising above it. Oh no, I'm not leaving … I have to. The kids are crying … they love me, crying over me and Georgia holding me in her arms and saying, 'don't die.' Shot in the stomach, below the heart. Shot for hiding people … other men. They're shooting them … they're all dead. I couldn't protect them."

As I brought Judy out of the trance, I was concerned she might be distressed by her past-life experience, ending with Anoir's violent death and the murder of his family. Judy opened her eyes, paused a moment, and then, as only she could, looked over to me and said, "What the fuck?

You didn't tell me that I could be male!" She'd assumed that if she had experienced a past life, she would have been female.

♦

This is the story of two people: me and my patient Judy. It tells of two very different lives that were destined to connect in ways that would change us forever.

Our stories begin when I first met Judy as a young psychiatrist, twenty-four years before she recounted her memory of Anoir. I had been working in private practice for only a few years, and I was admitting her to hospital. Judy was thirty-two and married, with a six-year-old daughter. She had been referred to me by another psychiatrist who had concerns over her ongoing risk of suicide. She had recently taken a potentially lethal overdose—not for the first time.

Judy walked slowly into the interview room in the hospital. She was wearing leggings and a floppy T-shirt, and slumped as she sat in the chair. She had darkish olive skin and looked older than her thirty-two years. Of low to average height, she was somewhat overweight and had jet-black hair. Both her hair and her weight were to change frequently in the future.

"Hi, Judy, I'm John Webber. I'll be the psychiatrist looking after you while you're in hospital. Can you tell me what's happened? I've read the letters from your doctors, but I need to hear the story from you."

"I'm fucked. My hand doesn't work. Look at it; it's useless."

Judy's hand was sitting limp on her lap.

"I can't do anything with it. How can I bring up Stacey without a right hand?"

"She's your daughter?"

"Yeah, she's six. At least she can dress herself now. I can't even sign my name. I have to write with my left hand. It's stupid. And it canes; the pain goes all the way up my arm and into my neck. I'm fucked. What's the point? Jonesy's sick of it."

"He's your husband?"

"Yeah."

"It would be good if I could meet him at some stage."

"Okay, but he's sick of it and I don't blame him. I'm fucked. I thought sixty tablets would do it for sure. It'll be more next time."

"You must have been feeling pretty desperate."

"Sometimes I take extra just to block it out, but I thought this would end it."

Judy was crying now and looked exhausted and sad.

"It's been a long time, hasn't it? It's four years since your original injury?"

"I told them I needed to change jobs. It just kept getting worse. But it's my fault."

"Why do you say that?"

"I don't know. It's just what I do. I fuck things up."

Four years earlier, Judy had suffered a wrist injury on a processing line at work. She had developed acute swelling of her wrist that needed emergency surgery. Despite the operation being described as successful, with no permanent damage to her nerves or tendons, she was unable to move her hand properly. In fact, she had lost nearly all the function of that right hand.

Judy's depression had been evident from the moment she walked into the room. As we talked her negativity, pessimism, and suicidal thinking were all obvious. She had lost interest in everything and felt guilty about all her perceived failings. She was anxious, agitated, and sleeping poorly.

"I'm mad," she said, "and nothing's worked."

She was right. She obviously had received a great many treatments and medications for all her symptoms, but without success. After the first operation, her severe and persistent pain required another, this time a surgical sympathectomy, which involved removing a rib and severing the sympathetic nerves that run along the spine and lead to the arm and head. Unfortunately, the surgery neither helped the pain nor improved the function of her hand. As well as the sympathectomy, she had twice had her wrist manipulated while under general anaesthetic. She had seen a rheumatologist and a rehabilitation specialist, attended a pain clinic, and received a lot of physiotherapy. She had seen psychiatrists and psychologists, and spent six weeks in a rehabilitation hospital receiving what was described as intensive counselling and more physiotherapy.

"And WorkCover reckon I'm faking it. As if I'd fake this. They keep checking on me, you know."

Judy had stopped crying and was now looking more anxious and fearful. She'd been on WorkCover since the injury; the insurance scheme covered her medical expenses and provided some ongoing income relief. It was paying for her to see me, as well as the cost of the private hospital, which she could not have afforded otherwise. It also required her to see independent doctors; patients were sometimes investigated by the system, especially if their case was unusual in some way, as Judy's certainly was.

"Well it doesn't look like you're faking it to me."

"I hate it. I can't even look after Stacey properly. I used to be a good cook, you know, but now even that's fucked."

"It's nice to hear you say something positive about yourself."

"But not now. I wouldn't care if they chopped it off."

Based on Judy's history, I thought the cause of her loss of hand movement was what is called a conversion disorder. These were common a hundred years ago, but rarely diagnosed in modern psychiatric practice. Freud described conversion disorders as the unconscious mind's attempt to deal with a problem for which the person can find no other solution. Talking to Judy, it wasn't hard to imagine that she had significant underlying stresses that were not immediately apparent. This was to prove somewhat of an understatement.

I was relieved to see that Judy's social situation seemed reasonably stable. She was living with Jonesy, who was Stacey's father. They weren't well off financially, but were managing. They lived in an outer suburb, nearly an hour's drive from where I worked. Judy had been employed at a local factory for a few years before her injury and had a number of close friends who lived nearby. Stacey attended the neighbourhood primary school. It wasn't obvious how well Judy's relationship with Jonesy had stood up to the past four years of her illness, but I had to assume it must have been difficult for Jonesy as well.

There hadn't been any apparent conflict at the factory, but as we discussed it, she declared, "My old friends at work, they dumped me. I reckon they're scared. The bosses are dark on me, and now they can't be seen to be my friend. John, they knew my wrist was getting worse. The nurses knew. They should've given me another job."

It wasn't easy getting a clear history from Judy, partly because of her depressed state but also because she was prone to jump from one topic to another. I wondered if she was consciously or unconsciously avoiding

Dr John Webber

certain subjects, or if perhaps it was due to her agitation and despair. Our first session ended with Judy still in tears. Her diagnoses had to include major depression, conversion disorder, and chronic pain but it wasn't at all clear what was causing her conversion disorder or why she had unconsciously chosen to lose the use of her hand. That her problems had persisted for four years, and if anything were getting worse, was a concern.

"We have to finish up today, but hopefully I'm going to be able to help in some way."

"But John, I don't know if you can. It's obvious—I'm mad."

Judy was certainly madly depressed, but she could have added madly scared, madly paranoid, madly in pain, madly confused, and mad at everyone including herself.

"Well, mad is what I'm supposed to deal with, so let's see how we go," I said as we left the room.

To be honest, if I were asked to look after Judy now, I would probably run a mile. At that time, though, I was young and perhaps overenthusiastic. All my training had been in public hospitals, where patients regularly presented with very complex problems. Such patients were also, like Judy, frequently from a more working-class background, and while I would not have admitted it, and was not proud of it, that also gave me a sense of academic or intellectual control, even superiority. So, with some feelings of familiarity combined with a little naivety and hubris, I pressed on, unaware of the anxieties Judy's case would create for me over the coming years.

While Judy remained in hospital, I delved into her past. The eighth of nine children, she'd had what was obviously a very difficult childhood, in a very rough and poor suburb of Melbourne.

"Mum was born in Australia but her parents were Italian."

That explains the olive skin, I thought.

"Did she have sisters and brothers?"

"Yeah, but John..." Judy had obviously chosen to call me John. "They were a bit snooty. They looked down on us."

"And your dad?"

"Brought up in one of those boys' homes. Never knew his parents. I don't think it was great for him. And my brothers were all retarded. Well, not really, only mild, you know—learning problems. They thought it was genetic. One day, on the way to hospital, I had to carry all my brothers' pee samples, you know, the whizz, and I accidentally dropped them. Piss everywhere. Shit, did I get into trouble for that. The genetic thing didn't affect girls, though."

"That must have been hard with eight brothers?"

"Yeah, it was."

Some time later, Judy told me she had seen a therapist as a child, and I wasn't surprised.

"That must have been hard on your parents too."

"The boys were forever getting into trouble. The police were always knocking on the front door. Then they'd search the house. Mum learned that the best place to hide them was in the ferret shed in the backyard. The police were never game to crawl in there! Sometimes, they were in there all day, and Mum would take meals out to them."

A slight smile would creep over Judy's face as she described this and similar events, and it was a relief for me to see a shift in her mood. It wasn't hard to imagine that even in the best of circumstances, Judy's parents would have been struggling with nine children, including eight disabled boys. More importantly, it was becoming apparent that Judy's early life must have been tough.

"And what about your schooling?"

"Well, I wasn't there much. My end-of-term reports, rather than recording how many days I had missed school, instead would say how many days I'd attended."

I was coming to admire Judy's wonderful sense of humour, though it barely surfaced during that first admission.

Marjorie, Judy's mother, had died quite suddenly and unexpectedly when Judy was fourteen. She collapsed in the driveway of their home, and Judy was the first to find her. As our initial sessions progressed, we talked about Judy's mother, and it became evident that Judy had not felt very loved or cared for by Marjorie. Judy painted a picture of her mother being quite disconnected, and completely preoccupied with the boys. I was surprised, although I shouldn't have been, by the sadness she still felt about her mother's death. As she described the events of that time, it was not hard to empathise with the despair and confusion she had felt as a young girl.

"Mum was always so sad. She seemed so unhappy," Judy said, "I had been saving money to give her a surprise night out on the town for her next birthday. She deserved a nice gift. I didn't want to be angry with her anymore."

I was sure Judy had hoped the gift might have created a closeness that had always been missing. By contrast, Judy described her relationship with her father as having always been positive. Presumably, she was the favoured daughter in a sea of struggling sons. She remained fond of her father, who lived in Melbourne. She admitted that he had been a big drinker and smoker and that his health wasn't good.

"He has to stay well," she said. "He's already had bypass surgery, you know, on his heart. But he's okay now."

"Has he stopped smoking?" I asked innocently, expecting her to say, "Of course."

"Not yet," she said. "He'll be okay. He has to be. I wouldn't cope if something happened to him."

"You mean, if he died?"

"Yeah, of course. Fuck, I can't even think about it."

Men, I presumed, were therefore going to have trouble living up to her father. Judy's relationship with her first husband, Patrick, had been short-lived. They met when she was eighteen. He had been in prison for armed robbery. Patrick also had a tough upbringing, spending most of his childhood in boys' homes, as Judy's father had. Judy met Patrick while visiting a cousin at the prison. They hit it off, and Judy continued to visit regularly. They decided to marry while Patrick was still in prison, when Judy was twenty-one. From my perspective, she had clearly been a bit mad even back then. Patrick came out of prison six months after the wedding, and they split up within two months. For Judy, it must have felt right, but only while he was in prison.

"Once he was out, I just couldn't cope. If I said I liked something, you know, like a piece of jewellery, there it would be, in its box, on my pillow at the end of the day. Jewellery, perfume, anything, but I don't think he always bought them! He was trying too hard. I knew it wasn't good for him either. It was too claustrophobic. I had to call it off. He never hurt me. It was just too much."

I'm not sure why she needed to tell me that he never hurt her, but it seemed important.

Over the course of her admission to hospital, Judy slowly improved.

Initially, I contemplated giving her ECT (electroconvulsive therapy), commonly known as shock treatment. I'd seen people respond wonderfully to this treatment, and it had to be considered, given the severity of her depression. It would have been a reasonable choice, but instead I decided to change her medications, involve her in some depression support groups, talk more, and see what happened with some rest and time out from the pressures of her chaotic life.

I hesitantly told Judy that I thought her loss of hand movement was a conversion disorder, and explained that when someone is extremely stressed, the brain can stop muscles working properly even though they aren't damaged. She was initially incredulous, and on more than one occasion asked me, "But John, how is that possible? I've only got three brain cells. So my three brain cells are causing that?"

And my answer had to be yes.

Her next question was, "And the pain?"

A tougher question, to which I could only respond, "Maybe."

"Bullshit, John, it really hurts!" was her reflexive response.

More of Judy's personality surfaced as she improved. Her thinking was very black and white, particularly in her opinions about people. It's probably already clear that her language was colourful to say the least, and when she described her situation and past events, I was never in doubt as to how she felt. Underneath that, there was also a very negative and critical view of herself.

Many of her traits and behaviours seemed contradictory. I've learned over the years that could be said for all of us. At times, she was angry and defensive, and at others disarmingly honest and frank. She could be very engaging, to the point of sometimes invading your personal space, but would quickly back off if asked. Once she was feeling better, getting her to stop talking or stay on topic wasn't easy. Then there was her sense of humour, usually at her own expense, but funny and probably a very important part of how she coped. She was mad as hell—but funny as hell too.

Judy was clearly very troubled, and yet there was a sense of energy about her. Despite my struggles with treating Judy, it was that engagement and energy that had me seeing her for years to come. She left hospital with her depression improved but still in pain. She still could not use her hand, and her jet-black hair was now purple.

At that time, there was no talk of spirituality. From the perspective of a young psychiatrist, firmly committed to his evidence-based medicine, spirituality was just another form of madness.

... ...

2. Discovering the past

In his thirties, my father-in-law, Brian, was hit by a double-decker bus while driving his prized Sunbeam Rapier car near the centre of Glasgow. The accident caused a small piece of metal to puncture his thoracic aorta. It was 1969, and only the early days of heart bypass surgery, but fortunately Mearnskirk Hospital in Glasgow had the equipment and expertise to provide the operation he needed, although they had only successfully performed it once before.

Brian vividly recollects that during the operation, he found himself floating up and out of his body. He hovered at what he thought was about ceiling height, looking down on the surgeons working on his opened chest. At the same time, he felt wonderfully at peace. There was no anxiety at all, and what he later described as a feeling of "no judgement." In that state, he remembers thinking to himself, "This is the real world—so what's that down there?" He then had the sensation that he was floating effortlessly over water towards a brilliant light.

Brian's next memory was waking up days later in the intensive-care unit with tubes and leads connected to all parts of his body. His case was written up in *The Lancet*, but no mention was made of his extraordinary experience. It happened well before renowned doctors Raymond Moody and Elizabeth Kübler-Ross started to write about near-death experiences.

From that time on Brian never had a fear of death. An accomplished engineer he remained actively engaged in life until his death, aged eighty-two. Over the intervening fifty years his memory of the event remained as vivid as it was initially.

I heard about Brian's story when I was going out with his daughter Kate, now my wife. I was a medical student, seriously attached to the science of my studies and quite dismissive of religion and related spiritual or metaphysical matters. At the time, I asked a more senior doctor what he thought of Brian's experience, and in response he said he understood it to be caused by a sudden release of neurotransmitters at a time of maximum cerebral stress. Good enough for me, I thought.

◆

Judy remained very unwell over the next decade. Because she didn't drive, she had to make the long trip to my rooms by train and tram, or talk a friend into driving her. Generally, her appointments were every two weeks, and although I would have preferred them to be weekly, the frequency depended a lot on her circumstances.

I explained to Judy that if her three brain cells could cause her conversion disorder, they could also fix it, and that her hand would improve if we continued to sort out her underlying problems and worries. That was easier said than done. The sessions were often chaotic, and her habit of jumping from one topic to another persisted. Whatever leapt into her head was the next thing from her mouth. It was like raking leaves in a storm. I often thought to myself, "You're the psychiatrist, John; you need to take better control of the session." Once, when I challenged her, she responded with, "I can't help it. It's like I've got six television programs on at the same time. Maybe I've got six brain cells?"

When she came to appointments, somehow Judy always seemed to be carrying two or three bags. She loved the discount stores and opportunity shops near my rooms, and would buy clothes and items for herself and Stacey. In one of the bags, there was usually a gift for me; it might be a Kit Kat or a quirky pen she liked. I tried to stop her giving me the gifts, saying I didn't need them and that it went against the ideals of therapy. She wouldn't hear of it, and might say, "Well, that's stupid. Anyway I'm a wog, you know, Italian, and that's what wogs do!" Eventually, I gave up. She liked that she was part Italian, and had enjoyed a good relationship with her Italian grandfather. The gifts were part of her identity, but also her way of thanking me for continuing to see her.

At the same time, Judy was always fearful that I would stop seeing her.

Dr John Webber

"One of these days you'll cuff me," she would say. "Everyone does." When saying "cuff," she would hold her left wrist up in front of her, as if looking at her watch, and then motion as if to brush off some annoying insect on the cuff of her sleeve. At times, her humour had a dark side.

"So, who are all these people who have cuffed you?" I asked during one of our sessions. "I know your mum died when you were young. Who else?"

"Well, she cuffed me from day one, really."

"And that's very hard on a young girl growing up." Maybe that was enough, I thought, but still asked, "And was there anyone else?"

"My grandfather died and, well, the women at work dumped me. Anyway, that's just what happens to me."

"I wonder if you think that happens to you because you don't deserve any better?"

"Exactly," Judy admitted.

"But why? What makes you so bad?" I asked. "Is it because—if your mum can't love you then who can?"

"Something like that," she said. "And now Dad's crook. I can't think about it. John, if something happened to him, I couldn't cope."

Judy visibly stiffened as she spoke.

"Because he loves you?" I asked.

"Absolutely. Like no one else did. And I love him. I was his little girl. I still am. You know, he once said to me that one day I would meet a man that I would love more than him. I hated him for that. As if I could love anyone else more."

"What about Jonesy?"

"Nope, not even close," she retorted.

The insights into her fears, I hoped, would be helpful, but often our discussions would become circular, and rarely did they seem to have any permanent impact.

Judy had also told me how upset she was when her previous psychiatrist had told her he could not see her fortnightly anymore: that he felt unable to get any further with her and would only see her monthly. Whatever his actual words had been, I wasn't about to judge him, as Judy wasn't making any sustained progress with me either. But what Judy revealed by telling me about it was how sensitive she was to any rejection or loss.

On occasion, Judy would bring her daughter, Stacey, to her

appointments. She was a cute little girl. A few times she came into the session, and it was nice to see they had a close bond. Usually, Stacey would stay in the waiting room and draw pictures or write letters to Judy or me while staff kept an eye on her. Sometimes she would slide a picture under the door to my consulting room. We would discuss her pictures at the end of the session and put them in Judy's file. I have no doubt Judy loved Stacey to bits and was very protective of her, but at the same time, I couldn't help but think that growing up with a mother who had Judy's problems would not have been easy.

During the first two years, Judy revealed more of her past. I discovered she had been through some extreme weight changes. By the age of eighteen or nineteen, her weight had peaked at twenty-six stone (165 kg). At the time, she was still living with her father, and had been told she would not survive long at that weight. She saw a psychiatrist and was assessed as being fit for surgery; as a result, she had gastric stapling.

"When I was in hospital, they had to take me downstairs to weigh me on the laundry scales. I was too heavy for the scales in the ward. Man, I should write a book—*Embarrassing Things I've Put Myself Through!*"

The gastric stapling resulted in dramatic weight loss and left Judy with large amounts of loose skin. Her abdominal apron (or spare tyre) was nearly down to her knees, so an apronectomy was performed, along with subsequent surgery to remove excess skin from her thighs. Before she became pregnant with Stacey, she'd also had a breast reduction because, as she put it, "everything was so out of proportion." At the end of describing all these surgeries, she noted, "The only thing they didn't do was my wings," at which point she held out her arms horizontally to reveal large flaps of skin hanging from her upper arms. "I still want these done, but James [her local doctor] won't let me."

Somewhat taken aback by the revealing of her "wings," I said: "Let's get that hand moving first."

"You still reckon it will get better?"

"Absolutely," I responded. "Tell me what happened after the staples and all that surgery."

It was so easy to get sidetracked with Judy.

"I lost heaps. If I ate too much, I chucked. I couldn't help it."

What Judy described then was a period of remarkable weight loss.

Already much slimmer, she met Jonesy, and by the time she was pregnant with Stacey, her weight had dropped to forty-three kilograms. As a consequence, she was hospitalised several times and received nasogastric feeding and additional intravenous supplements. She said they diagnosed her as having anorexia nervosa.

One of the psychiatrists she saw challenged her with the idea that she might be trying to kill her baby. Even in recounting this, Judy was horrified and exclaimed, "I just couldn't eat. I was really hurt that he would think that I could do that. John, there's no way. I was desperate to have a child but I never thought I could. My body was so fucked up. I'd never taken the pill. I didn't need to. I just figured it couldn't happen. So when it did, I was rapt. I just wanted someone I could really love and who would love me too."

Judy never held any resentment towards all the doctors and surgeons who had looked after her over those years. From her point of view, they had always been doing their best, had been respectful, and had probably saved her life. The paradox of that sentiment was not lost on me, given that she had on several occasions tried earnestly to kill herself.

When Judy wasn't coming to sessions, it was usually because I was treating her in hospital. During the first two years, I admitted her eight times, many more than I had anticipated and much more than I wanted for her or for her family. But each time it seemed critical, because of the depth of her depression, a major overdose, or the risk of suicide.

After another dangerous overdose, I elected to treat her with ECT. Despite all the complicating factors in her presentation, my training suggested that I had to see if it helped. I was optimistic that this might also help in reducing the amount of medication she was on. An earlier psychiatric report, from before I started seeing her, had commented on the "enormous" amount of medication she was taking and that it hadn't made any inroads. As it turned out the, ECT did help, but the improvement wasn't sustained.

So after two years, not much had changed. I was frustrated and so was Judy. Her hand wasn't getting any better, the pain was still bad, her periods of depression were profound, and she remained significantly at risk of killing herself. I wanted to reduce her medication and the frequency of her hospitalisations, and more than anything, I wanted to see her get better. Despite my feelings of therapeutic impotence, I still enjoyed my connection with her and knew she enjoyed seeing me. This was the silver lining, and I would remind myself that my therapeutic relationship with her was critical in the long term.

Around this time, Judy had missed quite a few appointments, and although I knew getting to them wasn't easy, I felt her explanations were a bit contrived. She was also looking very thin. So one morning I confronted her.

"Judy, you've missed quite a few appointments recently, and I'm not sure you're telling me everything."

"It's Jonesy," she said. "He's got worse."

Judy was looking out the window as if to disconnect from the topic being forced upon her.

"How do you mean?" I asked.

Judy forced her gaze back towards me.

"He's always been jealous, but he's really bad now. The other day I was talking to the pizza-delivery guy; he was a nice guy [it wasn't hard to imagine Judy having an engaging conversation with anyone], and Jonesy went berserk. I reckon he's worse when I lose weight, but I can't keep anything down. I'm having panic attacks. Feel like I'm going to faint. I can't even leave the house. I get up for Stacey, then go back to bed. It's fucked, John. He's really bad when he drinks."

"How did you get here today?"

"Maureen brought me."

Maureen was a close friend of Judy's, a great confidant and support who was to remain so over the coming years.

"And what happens when Jonesy goes berserk?"

"He hits me. He hits me really hard. The bruises … that's why I couldn't let you see. The other night, Madrina took me to hospital."

"What did they say?" Not my best response. I was stunned, and before she could answer, I tried again, "Judy that's terrible, what did they say?"

"I told them I fell."

"And they believed you?"

"Yep."

"Does anyone else know?"

"Madrina knows."

Madrina was an older lady who lived around the corner. Judy was very fond of her and her husband, Padrina, and had appointed them her godparents.

"She looks after me. She gets it."

"Judy, you could go to the police. You could press charges."

"I grew up with the police around all the time. It would just make things worse."

At that moment, I could hear the sound of an emergency vehicle in the distance. Perfect timing.

"Why didn't you tell me?"

Judy paused and thought for a while. She looked so sad.

"Because I'm mental. I fuck up everything. Why would you want to keep seeing someone who's that fucked up?"

"Because that's what I do. If I stopped seeing you because of what you just told me, *that* would be mental."

Judy went on to describe how Jonesy's drinking, jealousy, and physical abuse had gotten worse over the last four years. She had ended up in emergency on a few occasions, and each time she had convinced them (or maybe not) that it was accidental. If the bruises were still apparent, she would find an excuse to miss her appointment with me. Because she felt so bad about herself, she was convinced that I would only see her in the same light.

It raised so many questions. Why hadn't I been more alert to this possibility? I was aware that apart from Stacey, I hadn't met any members of the family: not her father or Jonesy. I had tried several times to see Jonesy, but without success. Was that because he had avoided it, or because Judy hadn't passed on the request? Probably both at different times, I thought.

I had no doubt that the abuse must be contributing to her depression, but was it also in some way linked to her conversion disorder—her hand paralysis? I had seen a woman many years before whose paralysis of her right arm had been triggered by her overpowering desire to kill her toxic mother. After all this time, could it be that Judy's paralysis was a consequence of her desire to kill Jonesy? Up until then, the only person she'd come close to killing was herself. So I had to ask, "Have you ever hit Jonesy?"

"You're kidding," she said. "He'd kill me."

I also had no doubt that Judy's description of Jonesy's abuse was real. I even got to see one of the more recent scars. Obviously, I couldn't make Judy do anything, but it was evident that the only solution was for Judy and Jonesy to separate.

With the help of friends, she finally left a few months later. There was no battle over custody—Stacey went with her. I was hopeful that this might open the door to some improvement. In the meantime, I needed to confront Judy's assumptions. If she saw herself as worthless and therefore deserving of abuse, then she almost certainly assumed that everyone else, including me, would see her in the same light. I knew there was a kernel of self-worth in there somewhere. Her warmth, frankness, individuality, and humour all appealed to me, and at some level, I knew these were things she liked about herself. She liked being a bit different—a bit mental. My challenge was to help her see those positives more often. If she could do that, sustained improvement might follow.

A year later, I had finally pinned down Judy's father for a meeting. Over the year, Judy had been struggling with the divorce and finding new accommodation for herself and Stacey. She'd had another admission during that time, and was now back in hospital recovering from an extreme period of depression. Again I had given her ECT, somewhat in desperation, as I knew it was effective in settling her quite quickly.

While Judy was still in hospital and recovering well, I arranged to meet her father in one of the interview rooms. Bernard appeared neatly dressed in tailored trousers and a checked shirt. He had a world-weary look on his face, but was obviously pleased to see Judy. I had expected him to be stocky, but he was wiry and not much taller than his daughter. Judy, for her part, was dressed quite colourfully, a sign that her depression was lifting.

"I'm pleased to meet you, Mr Bell," I said. "It will be helpful for me to get your thoughts on how Judy is going."

"She's looking a bit better now," he said.

"Yes, I agree," I said. "Judy usually picks up a fair bit with these spells in hospital."

"Yeah, and it must be bloody hard for her, not being able to use that hand."

That jolted me slightly. I was so used to Judy's hand paralysis that I would forget just how hard it must be for her. Not wanting to miss an opportunity to instil some optimism, I proffered, "I agree—I know it's been a long time, but I think there's still a good chance it will improve. There's still no strength, but she reckons it's moved a tiny bit recently, so we'll press on."

It became obvious that Bernard wasn't going to ask about Judy's treatments. I suspect he felt that wasn't his place.

"Judy tells me you've been unwell again this last year."

"Yeah, I had to have the bypass surgery again. It's okay though, now."

The doctor in me had the urge to ask about his smoking and drinking, but I knew it would have been at the end of a long line of previous warnings. Judy was still smoking a packet a day and was also looking down the barrel of vascular disease if she didn't stop. We'd had that discussion, and it was obvious she wasn't going to stop anytime soon.

As I talked to Bernard, Judy, who was sitting in the room with us, was saying virtually nothing, and that was most unusual. At that point, I also realised I was unlikely to hear any revelations from her dad. She clearly loved him, and he loved her, and for that reason, she was only ever likely to give him the sanitised version of what was going on, just as she had initially done with me regarding her marriage breakdown. In her mind, she couldn't afford to let those people close to her see the darker or seamier areas of her life, for fear of how they would judge her.

The rest of the meeting went well, and I knew Judy was pleased I had met her dad at last. As he walked away from us, down the corridor, Judy started talking again.

"You know he had gastric staples as well?"

"Really?"

"Yeah, he used to be pretty heavy, and he saw how much it helped me, so he had it done as well. He was a boxing instructor in the army, you know. That's why he became a security guard, and then he got too old for that and became a carpenter."

"Do you know what your mum did before she had kids?"

"Not really—but she worked for some mob called J. J. Gadsden's or something like that."

"Judy, I'm really pleased you're getting some movement in your hand. Even a little bit is a good sign. And I am pleased to have met your dad."

"Yeah, me too. Look, there's something else I have to ask you. One of the other patients said I was lucky to have you as my psychiatrist because you're one of the good-looking ones."

The subject wasn't completely new. I was aware that patients sometimes compared notes, and psychiatrists, while in hospital.

"John, I felt like belting her. It's a respect thing. So this is asexual, right?"

"Absolutely, and it's more than just respect, it would be wrong on so many levels. For starters, you could sue the pants off me [bad metaphor, I thought]. You would have every right to report me … but the most important thing is that if I let that happen it would be a complete betrayal of our relationship as a doctor and a patient. You need to be able to trust me, and that would be a huge abuse of that trust."

"Yeah, that's what I thought. Thanks."

And with that, Judy walked off down the corridor, ending the session herself for the first time I could remember. She seemed pleased. I didn't give it much more thought; that was just Judy being Judy, and I was pleased she was feeling better.

Bernard died six months later. Like a lot of deaths, it was expected and yet sudden. "I can't do it. It's too hard," she said to me in our first session after the funeral. She was devastated. Our previous discussions about how she might cope after he died, and about life and death in general, appeared to have done nothing to soften the blow.

"I know it's a cliché, but it's better to have loved him and now lost him than to have not had that love at all," I said. "And don't forget he had the benefit of you loving him; that's what you gave him."

"Fuck all that. I should have gone first."

"And how would that have left him feeling?"

Ignoring me, Judy said, "So now I can."

I wasn't going to win this argument, and nor did I want to make it one.

"Judy [I was starting to mimic her style of using her name every time I spoke to her], how can death be a solution to the problem?"

"No more pain."

I definitely wasn't going to win the argument. I wrote about her despair on the clipboard that always sat on my lap. It provided a moment of silence, and an opportunity to contemplate what I would say next.

"I can only imagine how sad you feel. I know I can't feel it the same way you're feeling it, but I know it must be terrible. It's normal to feel sad, and somehow you have to let yourself feel it and hang in there."

"So this is normal?"

"Actually, yes. It's exactly what I'd expect, and when you lose someone as important as your dad was to you, it takes a fair while to overcome it."

"I don't think I can do it."

"Well, I think you can. And you've got lots of people close to you."

"But they don't love me like dad did."

"And Stacey still needs…"

"Yeah, that'd be right—make me feel guilty."

I was never sure about playing the responsibility card, but right then I was desperate.

As I contemplated how I could best handle Judy's grief, I was aware that I had never suffered any significant grief myself. I had been born in New Zealand and came with my family to Australia when I was only two. All my relatives lived back in New Zealand, and travel was expensive, so I only saw my grandparents once or twice during my childhood. When I was about fourteen years old, my maternal grandfather died and I was told he'd suffered a burst aortic aneurysm when he was shopping downtown. "It would have happened very suddenly," were my mother's words. At the time, my feelings were more of curiosity than sadness, since I barely knew him. No one close to me had died, and so at a personal level, this sort of grief was foreign territory. In contrast, I had treated lots of grief and loss in my patients, and that experience would have to suffice.

It was no surprise that the next two years were punishing for Judy as she negotiated her grief. Like all grief, it reminded her of past losses: her mother, and little Cindy, who Judy had babysat many times when she was a teenager.

"She was the cutest little girl," Judy told me. "We used to love playing fantasies of living by the sea and going for swims and riding horses. I loved that. I've never ridden a horse you know. Her dad was never there. I don't know what he did, some sort of crook. And her mum, John, her mum was a scag, a real scag, doing all sorts of shit and always on the drugs. She had an older brother and sister but I really felt protective. I reckon she knew me better than her mum."

"What happened?"

"Her mum was out of it, as usual, and the brother and sister told her to stay while they went to get Red Rooster. But John, she was so little, and she followed them. They didn't realise; it wasn't really their fault. And then she tried to cross the main road on her own. It was always busy, even then. She got hit by a car. It killed her. I can't bear to think about it. I can't bear it. You see that's just fucking me up more!"

"You've never told me about Cindy before."

"Yeah I know … because it's too sad," Judy said, almost whispering as she wept.

Distracted by her own tears, I'm not sure if Judy saw the tears in my eyes. Trying to look calm, I wrote a few more notes as I wondered what was still yet to be revealed.

3. Born to suffer

Following the death of her father, Judy's hand continued to improve. She came in one day and, after placing her bags on the floor next to her chair, said, "Check this out!" as she pulled a cigarette out of its box. Normally, she would have put the cigarette box on her lap and used her bad hand as a weight on the box while she extracted the cigarette. On this occasion, she held the box between her legs, took the cigarette out with her good hand, wedged the cigarette between two fingers of the bad hand, and motioned as if to take a drag.

"That's brilliant," I spluttered. "Let's go downstairs and we'll talk while you smoke it."

I knew Judy had already smoked one, two, or three cigarettes outside while waiting for her appointment. I could usually smell it when she walked into my room.

"Shit no, not those stairs, my back's caning. Those stairs are a mongrel." Judy wasn't the first person to have complained about the flight of stairs up to my room.

"Alright, then, we'll do it at the end of the session."

Suddenly, cigarettes were part of Judy's cure. Over the coming months, Judy progressively developed more strength in that hand and started using a spoon. Eager to find something other than the cigarettes for her to work with, I was soon encouraging her to have soup as often as possible—anything that required a spoon. The improvement was slow, but it was real.

During that period of grief, Judy also finally told me about the sexual abuse she suffered as a child. She described it starting when she was very young and continuing until she was about fourteen, around the time her mother died. Five of her seven older brothers were involved. One in particular, Chris, was the ringleader. One of her earliest memories was of Chris fondling her with his hand down the front of her nappy. The abuse progressed to rape and, as Judy put it, "everything else." The worst times were when both parents were out, or nights when her mother was asleep and her father was at work or had passed out from drinking. On at least one occasion, Judy remembers her mother coming into the room when one of the brothers was forcing himself on her and then walking out without saying a word. The brothers would sometimes involve other boys or men in the neighbourhood. Chris made sure Judy wouldn't tell anyone by threatening to kill her father. Chris was much older, big and strong, and in Judy's mind was quite capable of killing her dad, or her for that matter.

Judy's abuse also extended to two of her uncles. One started when she was very young and the other began when she reached puberty. The second would comment on how much he liked her pubic hair. Again, Judy had been much too scared to say anything.

The hardest thing for me to hear about when Judy was describing the abuse was its ongoing and repetitive nature. In effect, she was living in fear all the time. If she was safe in any one moment, she knew she wouldn't be safe later in the day, or the next day. Psychiatrists know that people can sometimes make a good recovery from a single or even a few episodes of trauma, but Judy's abuse, starting from when she was very young, lasted most of her childhood.

Judy's brothers had always been protected by their mother, Marjorie, perhaps because of their disabilities, or because she saw them being less loved by their father. By the time Marjorie died, a number of the brothers had already moved out, one had died in an accident, and another was permanently crippled, apparently from a fight. Judy had also become big and angry enough to stop the abuse.

Whenever Judy was telling me about the sexual abuse, and in particular Chris's menace, it was hard to know whether her strongest emotion was fear or anger. Ultimately, I realised that it was neither: it was shame and guilt. Chris had repeatedly told her she was "born to suffer," and she could never completely get those words out of her head. Somehow, that also reinforced her belief that it must be her fault. When Judy talked about

Chris, she would always use his full name, Chris Bell. Somehow that helped, at least intellectually, to create a distance from him.

Recalling the details of the abuse and talking about it with me was really hard work for Judy. I was conscious of not wanting to re-traumatise her by asking to recount every horrifying detail, but at the same time, I wanted her to feel that she was safe in revealing what she could and expressing the feelings that had tortured her for so long. In truth, that part of the therapy never ended. It took years, partly because it was too distressing to tell all at once, partly because Judy needed to see how I responded, and partly, I think, because it was buried so deep that it took time to surface. Years later, when Judy was in her fifties, she described the routine she had created as a little girl to try and get herself to sleep.

"I knew one or more of the boys might come in at any time. So I'd stare at the wall—it was Housing Commission green—and imagine it was a beautiful violet-purple colour with paisley patterns. And while I looked at those beautiful patterns, I would sing to myself, 'Jeanie with the Light Brown Hair'."

Even in sleep Judy couldn't always escape, and often had a recurring nightmare.

"I'd be running with Dad. We were running away from the boys. Then Dad would fall in a deep hole, and no matter how hard I tried, I couldn't get him out of the hole, and the boys would get closer and closer. And then I'd wake up sweating like a pig."

As she described it to me, Judy was almost whispering, as if concerned that doing so too loudly might bring it all back or make it real again. The nightmare was easy to interpret, and clearly represented her fear that the boys would harm her or her father, but it also showed her feelings of responsibility towards her father. My job now was to help Judy cope with actually losing him, and to somehow shift her belief that the abuse had been all of her own making.

"Judy, you understand, don't you, that children always tend to blame themselves. When something bad happens, they naturally assume it is their fault. I know that little girl isn't to blame. She is completely innocent. It's not her fault."

"I know it's fucked; it's just how I feel."

"Imagine … if little Cindy had been sexually abused, would you have said it was her fault?"

"That's not fair. She was beautiful. I was…"

"You were what, Judy, a beautiful little girl as well?"

"It's just like—that's the way it was. I was born to suffer," Judy said, crying. "It's how it was. I know it's fucked; it's just how it is."

"It's not how it is now, Judy. At least now we can look at it differently. You can look at it differently."

Some part of Judy could see the logic of all that, but another part still blamed herself and saw herself as deserving the worst. This self-loathing had been hard-wired since childhood. During that session, I couldn't help myself, and had to ask, "Were there any other recurring dreams?"

"The other one was just as bad. Mum would be in the boys' room, sitting on top of one of the bunks. Some of the boys would be on their bunks as well. Then Mum would throw pieces of a broken mirror at me and tell me to get her a glass of water. I'd get her the water but she'd keep throwing pieces of the mirror at me. Pretty fucked up, eh?"

Judy understood this dream as representing her mother's continuing attack on her no matter what she did. A more extraordinary interpretation would have been that it represented Judy's unconscious insight that Marjorie couldn't bear looking at herself, and by throwing pieces of mirror was blaming Judy for her failings as a mother.

Other aspects of her childhood surfaced during those sessions.

"Grandpa made me feel good," Judy told me. "He talked a lot about Italy and all the old ways. I don't think he was very happy. I didn't like Grandma and Mum's older sisters. A bit snooty, John, you know. A bit 'we're better than you.' But Grandpa was cool."

"You like having a bit of Italian in you, don't you?"

"Yeah, it's the duck's nuts. I'm a wog. I like that."

Judy also spoke more of her parents.

"I loved Dad, but I know he wasn't perfect. He could be pretty mean and rough with the boys. He would make them wrestle with him but then go too far."

Both he and your mum did a lousy job of protecting you, I thought to myself.

"I know he used to pass out at night from the drinking, but what was he like when he drank?"

"Yeah, he could be pretty hard on Mum."

"How do you mean?"

"Sundays, John, it was epic theatre on the telly, and then epic theatre in the kitchen. After Sunday school [I'm sure my eyebrows raised, as I was a bit shocked she went to Sunday school], we'd watch one of the old epic movies on telly. You know, Romans, gladiators, and battles? Then after lunch, after Dad had too much, it was epic theatre again, and he'd start hitting Mum and calling her a black bastard. I don't understand why he called her that, but me and the boys wouldn't hang around to watch. It was fucked. Scary shit, John."

As a child, I had briefly attended Sunday school, but my only memory of it was walking home and picking mint from someone's front garden, which Mum would make into sauce for the Sunday roast. It certainly wasn't scary shit, though Dad occasionally thumped his hand on the table and told us to sit up straight and hold our knives properly.

I pondered how Judy could hold such affection for a man who was so brutal, but had to accept that she felt love from him. Why wouldn't a little girl in her situation take love wherever she could find it?

"You know, sometimes Mum would let me come into her bed with her."

I was keeping quiet, but I liked the idea that Judy could get into bed with her mum, at least implying that there were some moments of affection or intimacy.

"Sometimes she'd ask me if she could pinch me, and I'd say yes. And then she'd pinch me so hard it really hurt. Then she'd say, 'We always hurt the ones we love.' I didn't get it … but I always let her do it. Why would she do that?"

The furrows on Judy's forehead had deepened as she verbalised her confusion over her mother's behaviour. I had a thousand possible explanations running around in my head. For Marjorie, love and pain were inseparable, and this was her perverse means of showing affection. At the time, my best answer was, "Maybe when you let her pinch you, it made her feel that you loved her?" I wondered more about Marjorie's upbringing and whether she had suffered any abuse. Many years later, Judy told me her mum had long scars over her back from when her mother used to thrash her.

Judy was still talking:

"John, one morning when I was in bed with Mum, Dad came home early from his night shift and got into bed with us. I expected him to touch me, you know, sexually, but he didn't, John. He didn't. He never did."

When I considered the sexual and physical abuse that Judy had suffered and the abuse she had witnessed, I thought, no wonder she was initially attracted to a man who was safely in prison. No wonder she put on so much weight that men would not be interested in her sexually, and then go in the other direction and lose extraordinary amounts of weight, perhaps in the hope that she would become invisible. No wonder she couldn't tell me about her abuse at home while her dad remained alive, worried that her brother Chris, whom she still feared, might kill her or her father. In the end, given how much she blamed herself and how ashamed she felt, it was no wonder she couldn't tell me, for fear I would see her in the same light—as a person unworthy of love, who was born to suffer.

I hoped that talking about the abuse might be therapeutic, like releasing the pus from an abscess, but often all it seemed to leave was a gaping hole. Some sessions she would come in crying and was still crying when she left. There was sadness for a lost childhood, and now years of her adult life that were a wreck. I preferred it when Judy was angry—that was at least better than despair. And the anger then was towards her abusers rather than at herself. Most of all, Judy had finally allowed herself to talk about the abuse, and in the process had taken the leap of trusting me. Our shared knowledge of the abuse could now be used as a new foundation for future sessions.

The risk of suicide remained, and I would admit Judy to hospital when I was most fearful. One of those admissions was following a huge overdose. Judy had taken two hundred and fifty tablets, and had spent several days in intensive care. On that occasion, the overdose had included a lot of Panadeine, which had damaged her liver, and the doctors were concerned she would go into liver failure. She didn't, and I remember being grateful she wasn't also a drinker.

After that episode, Judy settled, but James, her local doctor, had recently warned me she might be hoarding tablets again. As a consequence,

I challenged her. "Judy, James and I are worried you might be keeping a pile of tablets you could overdose on," I said. On this particular day, Judy was more dishevelled and disorganised than usual. Her hand and associated pain were continuing to improve but she was having more and more trouble with back pain. A recent scan had shown severe degeneration of her lower back. On James's recommendation, she was now using a walking stick, but somehow still managed to bring two bags into the room with her.

"You know I have to keep some tablets, in case?"

"Yes, but not a great pile of them."

"Yeah, but if it gets too hard, I just need it there. It's hard, John, sometimes it gets too much. They're still watching me, you know."

"Who? WorkCover?" Nice change of topic, I thought.

"Yeah, I know their van." She said this with a mixture of fear and anger in her eyes.

A short time ago, I had written to James about the WorkCover (insurance) problem. Judy had been required to attend yet another review by an independent psychiatrist. These were always very stressful for Judy, as she assumed they would conclude that there was nothing wrong or that she was faking it. Invariably, their assessments supported her case despite her improving arm, and usually remarked on the chronicity and severity of her illness and their pessimism regarding her prognosis. I noted to James, "She has become increasingly suspicious that she is being followed and watched. This may of course be true, at least some of the time." The WorkCover system was a poisoned chalice. While it paid for me, and her admissions to hospital, Judy perceived its processes as an attack on her, and this certainly wasn't the first time we had talked about it.

"Judy, we'll get back to that."

"And John, John [two Johns meant she was serious and I really needed to pay attention], Stacey's been seeing boys. John, she's hanging around with some real losers, bad families [the irony of that wasn't lost on me], and they're bad John; I have to protect her."

Judy saw her primary role in motherhood as protecting Stacey from any form of abuse.

"Judy, Stacey is fifteen now. She's naturally going to be interested in boys."

"Nuh, I can't handle it."

"So have you talked about sex with her?"

"Yeah, of course, everything. You know what Mum told me about sex? That sex was like a milkshake. That was it. I didn't get it. I still don't."

"I agree I have no idea what that means. So have you talked to Stacey about condoms and contraception?"

"John, that's the most important bit."

"Does she see James?"

"Yep."

"Okay, that's cool."

At least she had a good doctor she could see if needed. I didn't push the issue, but I knew that Judy's illnesses and absences had made Stacey's upbringing far from ideal.

"Judy, all you can do is offer her the best advice and support you can."

"But sometimes she won't talk to me."

"Well, that's pretty normal too."

By the end of the session, I had got back to the original topic and made Judy promise she would bring her stash of tablets to the next session, which she did.

This session reminded me of the words of an old mentor, John Cone, a psychiatrist who specialised in family therapy. Sometimes after we had seen a particularly remarkable or pathological family, we trainees would excitedly discuss the fascinating dynamics that had been on show. Dr Cone would remind us that in psychiatry, it was easy to become a voyeur and forget we were there to treat the patient. So it was with Judy; there were times when I was transfixed by her frightening and tumultuous story, and needed to remind myself that she was there to be helped.

A session two months later was no exception. It was a warm day in Melbourne, so Judy was dressed more lightly than usual and more of her tattoos were showing. It wasn't that long ago that Judy had delivered me her stash, so I thought I would pursue the history of her drug-taking. I knew she smoked dope, mostly bongs now, and that her use of medication was often not as prescribed. I also knew she occasionally used heroin when things got bad, though her finances limited her use. Issues surrounding Stacey were pressing, so we talked about that first. Then I posed the question.

"Judy, you know I'm always worried about what drugs you're taking, but I'm vague about when you started. When did you start?"

"When I was a kid."

"Yes, but when? How old were you?"

"When I was five or maybe four. I used to take Mum's Mandrax. I knew it bombed her out, so I tried it."

"Jesus, that could have killed you!"

Mandrax, no longer available, was a barbituate-like drug that had a respiratory-depressant effect, and could have been fatal for a child of that age.

Judy continued, unaffected by my alarm. "It worked, it knocked me out, and if the boys came in, I never remembered it. I couldn't do it too much, because she could tell they were missing."

Some days, it seemed, you were better off not asking the question.

"Chris Bell gave me my first joint when I was seven," she told me. "I think that was before my first fag. He wanted to see what effect it had on me. He also gave me my first needle. I reckon I was about eleven. John, I still couldn't say no. But if he hadn't, someone else would have. Everyone tried it."

"Do you reckon you've ever been addicted?"

"Nah, couldn't afford it. John, I'm ashamed, I don't like talking about it, but it's nice sometimes; it just takes me away."

The summer progressed, and a few sessions later, Judy, now at the heavier end of her weight range, was coughing a lot. I thought to myself, I'm never going to stop her smoking. She was also sporting a new hairstyle, completely shaved on one side and shortish, but styled on the other.

"What do ya reckon?" she asked, but went on before I could answer. "You see, this side is where they did the sympathectomy, and it doesn't sweat at all, so I can keep it longer, and this side sweats like crazy, so I had it shaved. I like it. Whaddya think?"

"Yes, I like it. [As if I had a choice.] It's very different. It suits you."

"Exactly."

"John, I'm thinking about giving up WorkCover. I'm over it. I can't deal with it. They've sent me an offer and made me see a lawyer. Ian's [her solicitor] looked at it. He reckons I should do it. Look, what do you think?"

Judy searched deeply into one of her bags. After saying "fuck" three times and digging into the other bag, she pulled out a crumpled piece of paper with calculations as to her payout. It was complicated. I explained that if she excepted the payout, I would bulk-bill her fee, which meant a significant drop in payment for me but no out-of-pocket payment for Judy. If she was careful with her money and took out private health insurance, I would still be able to admit her to hospital.

"Judy, it's really hard for me to advise you, but I think you should do it." I wanted to shout, "Take it! The system's been driving you crazy for years." We had previously talked about this issue at length. There was still some pain in her arm, but the hand was close to fully recovered. She still obviously had severe episodes of depression, but there were now multiple explanations for that, not just the work injury.

"Judy, if you were off it, you could stop feeling like you are being watched all the time. And stop feeling judged by them."

"But, John," Judy said, now with tears in her eyes, "I reckon then you'll cuff me. I can't help it. I just know that's what happens."

Judy had only ever seen me under that old system, and in her mind, any change could destroy that. I reached over to Judy's file on the table next to my chair. It was big and heavy. I checked the date of when I first saw her.

"Judy, I want you to really pay attention to what I'm going to say. I've now been seeing you for ten years. I like seeing you. I like treating you. You drive me crazy, but I love your sense of humour, and I love that you are different. So unless I croak, I'm not going anywhere."

"You'd better not fucking croak, then." Judy usually got the last word in even if it was while she was walking down the stairs.

Over those ten years, I had admitted Judy to hospital seventeen times. She had taken five dangerous overdoses, been treated with ECT on several occasions, and been prescribed a wide range of psychiatry's pharmacopeia. I had sought second opinions from other psychiatrists on occasion, but while these had been helpful, they had done little to effect a recovery. Exploring Judy's problems was like heading down an endless rabbit hole. I wasn't about to give up on her, but I felt the weight of responsibility, and to be honest I wouldn't have minded a break.

As the old saying goes, "Be careful what you wish for, for you may surely get it." It was four months before I saw Judy again. Two weeks after that session, she was admitted to an intensive-care unit, not from an overdose, but suffering from Guillain-Barré syndrome, a rare autoimmune disease that causes muscle paralysis and can be fatal when severe. I was told it involved all her muscles and she required ventilation with a respirator. Her recovery would be slow.

4. Alone again

"I was floating up in the corner of the room, right up, looking down on my body with the machine pumping my lungs up and down. Then there was a beautiful gold light, John, just over my left shoulder, a gold light like you've never seen before, And it was telling me that it wasn't my time yet, that I still had to look after the kids. I should've looked around; I didn't, but I wasn't scared. I felt so calm, so peaceful. But I don't understand. John, it doesn't make sense; I've only got Stacey and I can't have any more."

Judy knew she couldn't have more children as she'd had an endometrial ablation, soon after the birth of Stacey, which rendered her infertile. So the mention of kids—plural—was confusing. What she didn't know was that Stacey, now fifteen, who had been keeping vigil at her bedside, would be pregnant in twelve months' time with the first of four grandchildren to come.

♦

Four months had passed, and Judy, making more ruckus than usual, charged into the downstairs consulting room, if charging is possible when you are walking with a frame.

"John, thank God, I made it. Fuck me, what a trip, John, it was a complete spin. I thought for a while it was the Maggot Motel for me, you know, the Box Condo. They said I might not walk again, but look at me."

Judy said all this before she even sat down.

"Judy, I'm really pleased to see you. Now have a seat and tell me what happened, from the start."

"You know I had bronchitis when I last saw you. Well, I just got sicker. I was getting weaker and weaker. Like, everything, my arms, my legs, even talking was hard … yeah, don't you say anything." She humorously pointed an accusatory finger at me. She was right: I wasn't going to pass up the opportunity to applaud an occasion when she was less able to talk.

"John, cop this: I thought it might have been another conversion but this time, not just the hand … everywhere. It just got worse."

Judy then went on to describe how she had floated up into the corner of the room and not understood the message she had received.

"John, it's a bit 'nee-nor nee-nor,' you know, *Twilight Zone*."

"You know, my father-in-law had a similar thing when he was really sick," I replied. "Apparently, it's got something to do with a massive release of neurotransmitters when you are close to death. Now, tell me, what's happened since then?"

That was all the airtime I allowed Judy to give that out-of-body, gold-light experience, but it was not the only time this was to happen to her. Eventually, my understanding would be transformed by an appreciation that an event like this could be life-changing, as it had been for my father-in-law. At the time, from my point of view, Judy had bigger fish to fry.

Judy went on to describe recent events. Not all of her recounting was decipherable, as there were the usual four or five sub-plots being conveyed at the same time. Fortunately, I had discharge summaries from the hospitals and a letter from James. I learned that Judy had spent most of the last two months in a rehabilitation hospital and had returned home only a few weeks ago.

Everything was a mess. Judy was still very weak and had a lot of pain. "It hurts everywhere. Everything is so stiff. It hurts when I move. It's a sharp pain." Judy was still obviously disabled and was probably not attending rehab as often as she should. Stacey had been looked after by a Christian group, which billeted her with families while Judy was in hospital, but was still, according to Judy, hanging out with the wrong boys.

I was always worried about Stacey. She had endured a very difficult upbringing, and must have witnessed some of Jonesy's violence towards Judy. She had also been forced to cope with times when Judy spent days

Dr John Webber

in bed, refusing to leave the house, fearful she was being videoed, or times when Judy had self-medicated and was in a haze. On one occasion, she had found Judy unconscious after an overdose. In that instance, Stacey was supposed to have stayed the night at a friend's house, but came home for something she'd forgotten. In addition to all that, she'd had to survive long periods when Judy was in hospital. So Stacey's attachment to Judy would have always been riddled with the fear of losing her mum. She must also have been aware, at some level, of Judy's dependence on her. On the occasions when I saw her, I always attempted to reinforce that she was not in any way responsible for her mother's illness, and hopefully that was helpful. The problem now was that Stacey was starting to spread her wings and find some independence. Judy was smart; she knew it was inevitable. But that didn't mean she had to like it.

Maureen, Judy's loyal friend, had again brought Judy to her appointment that day. She had previously worked as a teacher, but had become more interested in herbal and natural remedies—'hoogey-jus,' as Judy called them. Maureen had her own family woes, and according to Judy received little help from her husband, 'Born-Again Barry' who was too busy praying. I was certainly grateful for Maureen's efforts.

We were moving towards winter now, and Judy's hair was longer and less lopsided, but with a dramatic red streak. She was thin again, perhaps because of the Guillain-Barré syndrome, the stress of Stacey's growing independence, or perhaps something else? I wasn't always the quickest study, but I had learned not to jump to conclusions where Judy was concerned.

"Judy, you are looking pretty thin."

"John, I can't keep anything down. It's the staples. I used to be able to keep it down, you know, stop it from coming back up, but now the muscles are too weak and it just comes back up."

"Can you keep fluids down?"

"Yeah, sort of."

"Try soups—stick them in the blender—at least until you get stronger?"

Such were the sessions sometimes. I always hoped we might spend more time on Judy's self-recriminatory thoughts and feelings. My goal was to help her put the past in perspective and be less damning of herself, and to find strategies to deal with her fears and the negativity that took over during her bouts of depression. But despite my best efforts, the immediacy of Judy's current problems often dominated the hour. At the end of the session, as I put the notes I'd written into her file, I finally asked about WorkCover. Had she taken their offer of a lump-sum payment and gotten out from under their scrutiny?

"John, I couldn't do it. Not yet, anyway. It would have been too hard."

◆

Over the next ten years, Judy remained very unwell. Eventually, WorkCover refused to pay. They concluded that other factors were dominant in her illness, and they were probably right. She eventually had her staples out because of the vomiting it caused. Many aspects of Judy's psychological struggle were to remain the same, but many things were to change. Her hair, of course, was always changing.

◆

Three months on from her first consultation after the Guillian-Barré syndrome, Judy decided to move house as a consequence of all her frustrations. I was not at all convinced it was sensible.

"Judy, you know the old saying, 'If you run away, you just take yourself with you'?"

I knew that didn't invariably apply; I'd certainly had patients whose move away from a toxic environment had been helpful. But I knew Judy's problems were primarily internal, not external. Moving also meant potentially moving away from all the people who had supported her. I had always been grateful that I could share the responsibility for Judy with James, her local mental-health team, and friends like Maureen who had stuck by her and helped her care for Stacey.

"John, every time I walk out the front door, I can see the factory [where she had suffered the original injury]. And Stacey's hanging out with the wrong guys."

I couldn't stop her, and in the end I knew it was her decision to make. With Stacey, she moved several suburbs away to where Melbourne's urban sprawl was slowly encroaching on what had been farmland and country towns. It meant she lost all her local supports, including James.

The move was a disaster, but not in the way I expected. Apart from her ongoing emotional and physical problems, Judy's heroin use escalated. She was ashamed and for a while avoided telling me, but it became too much to hide. Judy was now injecting heroin daily. She found a new local doctor, Tom, who summarised the situation beautifully in a letter he wrote to me: "Judy has been seeing me regularly recently and I believe she has broached the issue of her heroin use and methadone treatment, about which she was initially reticent because she did not wish to lose your respect and care." As always, Judy's fear was that I would use the problem as an opportunity to "cuff" her.

When I first realised the extent of her heroin use, I asked, "What happened? How did it take over?"

"I just couldn't cope with the pain anymore, with any of it; it just gets too much. And John, it's so easy to get it where I am now. There're dealers everywhere; half of the time it's free."

"And Stacey?"

"No way; I don't let her see it."

"Really?"

"No, really, and John, she's hanging around with losers."

"That sounds a bit hypocritical, given who you must be dealing with."

"No, that's not fair, I'm just using it for the pain. It helps me cope. John, my brain goes quiet for a while."

"Judy, you know I'll keep seeing you, but this is not my territory. You need to get help from the right people."

Drug addiction was not my area of expertise. Its treatment invariably involved specialised clinics and involvement with organisations like Narcotics Anonymous. Fortunately and ironically, one of Judy's great strengths had always been her resourcefulness, and in particular her capacity to connect with people, as she had done with me. This had always been one of the great contradictions about Judy. My own father would have affectionately called her "as rough as guts," but despite this and her own self-loathing, she remained incorrigibly extroverted and likeable. As a result, she had found Tom, attended Narcotics Anonymous, and stayed on methadone for a year.

During this time, Stacey, still living with Judy, became pregnant and, at nearly seventeen, gave birth to Dylan. Judy was still recovering from the Guillain-Barré syndrome and suffering severe bouts of depression, and often needed admissions to hospital. Her heroin use remained a problem, and now she had baby Dylan joining her, Stacey and Travis at home. God, she was complicated! The never-ending, chaotic, and spectacularly colourful nature of Judy's problems usually galvanised me, but given their intractability, there were times when I felt therapeutically bereft and was at risk of becoming numbed or even complacent. That was particularly true during her period of heroin addiction. Fortunately, while Dylan's arrival complicated matters even more, it renewed my focus.

I saw Judy soon after Dylan's birth. By now she had progressed to using a walking stick, was still thin, and her hair was remarkably plain.

"It reminds me of when Stacey was born," she said, as she spoke lyrically about Dylan. "He's beautiful, and Stacey's doin' okay. She's still pretty sore, but John, Travis [Dylan's father] is a scumbag. He's scary, John. I know I have to shut up, but … I don't trust him."

"How about you? How are you travelling?"

"Yeah, okay."

"And the methadone?"

"Oh, John, it's a pain. I have to go every day … every day!"

"To pick up your dose?"

"Yeah, of course, and sometimes the way they stare at you … like you've crawled out of the gutter."

A look of disgust came over Judy's face as she watched me intently, expecting to see the same disdain on my face.

"That sounds more like the way you see yourself?"

"Yeah, maybe. But one of them looks at me like that. I can tell."

"You'll get there. One day, you'll look back on the heroin and say, 'What was I thinking?' And I reckon somewhere down the track, you'll even be feeling better about yourself."

"Oh sure, like I'm just a bit crap, not total crap."

"Well, that's a start. I know there are times when you feel better about yourself. We just have to keep working in that direction."

About a year later, Judy, now off methadone but still struggling with using too much heroin, found a Christian group called Teen Challenge, which ran a live-in drug rehabilitation facility. They were fundamentalist in their approach to religion, and against nearly all medication, including psychiatric medication. *Especially* psychiatric medication. They were also against any form of psychiatric treatment. Despite that, Judy, in her inscrutable way, had convinced them to let her continue her medication and attend her appointments with me.

"John, there's a lot of God talk," she said during one of those appointments. "And we have to read the Bible. And then they test us. And they make us get up in the morning. And it's really strict. No contact with the males except at four o'clock. I'm in a room with Sandra and she's nice. And, John, no cigarettes."

"So no cigarettes, no dope, no heroin, since you've been there?"

"I know ... amazing."

I had to admit it was working well. Judy was obviously missing Stacey and Dylan, but it was working. Against the group's advice, Judy finally left after three and a half months.

"John, during one of the meetings, they asked us, 'What was the worst thing that had ever happened to you?' I told them about the baby with the blood in the nappy, and then they asked, 'What did you think God was doing when that was happening?' and I said, 'I'm fucked if I know, not much obviously.' Then they said, 'He was in the corner of the room crying.' Well, that did it. I was out of there."

From that time on, Judy was to remain off the heroin, apart from using it very occasionally, as she had in the past, when she was desperate. Her use of cigarettes and marijuana quickly returned to their previous levels.

When Judy returned home after Teen Challenge, she felt compelled to help Stacey and Dylan but living with Travis was difficult and never going to last. It was an uneasy truce. Eventually, Stacey moved a few suburbs away, and Judy moved into a unit on her own.

Over the next eight years, Judy's state of mind would be strongly influenced by where and how she lived, and in particular her relationship with Stacey, young Dylan, and the future grandchildren. In our sessions, Judy described how much she hated living alone.

"John, I've never lived on my own," she explained one day. "I lived with Dad until I moved in with Jonesy. Sometimes when I was babysitting, I lived with a family while their father was in jail, but I was never on my own. And Patrick lived with me and Dad before we split up."

"Maybe it's important for Stacey to do it on her own? It makes sense that she have a go at being…"

"But I rarely see her … or Dylan."

"Maybe it could be good for you too?"

"John, you're not listening. What if he [Travis] hurts Dylan?"

As I shifted in my chair, I wondered if I was naive. I could only remember receiving one clip over the ear during my childhood, for hurting my sister while jostling with her over a bicycle.

"Judy, you know you can't control everything. Stacey has to live her own life."

"John, I couldn't bear the thought of something happening to Dylan, or Stacey."

"Yes, I know."

I was struggling, and probably for that reason, or perhaps because Judy had mentioned her childhood, I asked, "Judy, did you ever have holidays when you were a kid?"

"Now *you're* mental. As if that ever happened. Sometimes I used to stay with Granddad, you know, Pop Deluca? I liked that. Especially if Grandma was busy. She didn't like me; we were trash. Grandad was nice. He talked about Italy and life there. And sometimes we'd go to French Island. You know, on a boat, to the prison on French Island. We would visit the boys when they were there. They'd take us over on the boat and tell us that the water was full of sharks."

I wasn't sure if Judy enjoyed the trips because of the boat ride or because one or more of the boys was in prison. As if reading my mind, she then said, "They didn't all abuse me, you know, just five of them. You could tell how old each one was depending on which prison. First it was Turana, then French Island, and then Malmsbury in the country, or Pentridge. So, did you have holidays?"

I was a bit shocked. It wasn't like Judy to ask me about my own life, and I preferred to keep that private, but I felt it was important to answer her question.

"Actually, I did. We had holidays down at the beach, and up at a farm owned by one of my father's friends. They were great. I was lucky."

One of the other likeable things about Judy was that she never showed any resentment for what others had. She just liked the idea of having fun, and her idea of fun always meant being with others. I wondered if that's why she did so well at Teen Challenge, but right now she felt very alone and was clearly distressed.

At the end of the session, I remained worried. I had often reminded her that she could ring the practice if she needed to, but she had always been very respectful and only rang occasionally.

"Judy, you know you can ring me if you need to?"

"John, I've got you on speed dial at home. You're the first three, the first one is 'Doc,' then 'His Royal Highness,' and then 'God'."

I couldn't help but chuckle and smile broadly. Sometimes, Judy was just funny; this time she was funny and cheeky. I knew it was meant as a compliment, but it made me nervous being up on a pedestal. There was too much risk of falling. I'll have to tell Kate (my wife) about the speed dial, I thought to myself. It wouldn't be the first time I had come home with a humorous Judy anecdote. She was by far the commonest source of such stories. In truth, I was struggling with Judy's continued ill health and suicide risk and offloading to Kate provided some release. She was receptive because she knew I wouldn't normally discuss my patients unless they were really troubling, or funny.

"Judy, one of these days your humour will be your undoing," I then offered.

"What do you mean?"

"Actually, I'm not really sure … but what I need to know is that you are safe—that you will get help or ring me if you need to."

During the session, we had also discussed the options of calling the crisis-assessment team, or taking herself to emergency, or calling Maureen or even Lifeline.

My concern now was that Judy was no longer on WorkCover, so I could no longer admit her to hospital under my care. She also wasn't sick enough to be certified and forced into hospital, so I had to rely on the public mental-health services, which were unlikely to admit people unless the circumstances were dire.

By the end of the session, I wasn't convinced I had extracted a comprehensive promise that she wouldn't harm herself, and so I again repeated, "Okay, so no hurting yourself and no overdoses."

Judy remained safe over the next two months, but soon after, while still living alone and seeing less of Stacey and Dylan, she took another massive overdose. She spent days in intensive care, and once required cardiac resuscitation. From there, she went on to be treated at a public psychiatric hospital and was given a further course of ECT.

When I first saw her after all those treatments, she was still surprised the overdose hadn't killed her.

"John, I can't believe it. I figured if I took three hundred and sixty-five tablets, one for every day of the year, it had to work."

I had felt devastated when I heard about Judy's overdose. I was sad that she felt so alone and so desperate. I was distressed at the thought that I could have lost someone I was very fond of. Selfishly, I felt hurt that she could do that to me after I had been so involved with her over the previous fourteen years, and at a professional level I felt I had failed. Her illness was serious and chronic, but platitudes like this gave little solace. I was also frustrated, because I always felt that with the right treatment Judy had the potential to find more continuous peace of mind.

"How are you feeling now?"

"Yeah, a bit better, but I still can't believe it. And John, I had the gold light again. I was up in the corner of the room, on top of everything. It's so beautiful, and over the left shoulder again. And I could see what was happening. It was really bright where I was, but darker down where they were working on me."

An odd sense of calm and clarity came over Judy as she described these events.

"They were using the paddles on me. It was so beautiful, and it was like I was talking to the light. It was like I knew I couldn't die because I had things to do. But John, here's the kicker. The overdose included heaps of quinine. I couldn't see or hear for days when I woke up. Apparently quinine does that. They thought I might stay blind."

"No more quinine?"

"Shit no; I'll have to find something else for the cramps."

"That all sounds extraordinary, and I am really pleased to see you, but Judy, I need you to know I've been really upset by how close you came to dying. And it's not just me. It would have had a huge effect on Stacey and all your friends."

"But John, I didn't use any of your tablets—they were all from the other doctors. Don't make me feel bad."

"I don't want to make you feel bad but I needed you to know that."

I didn't know where to go with the tablet revelations. In many ways, which tablets she took was irrelevant, but I knew it was important to her, and I needed to use that influence to prevent her doing it again. So I said, "I really appreciate you not using my tablets but I just need you to not do it again. No more overdoses!"

Once more, I did not pursue Judy's near-death experience. Regardless of what she saw and despite her loss of vision and hearing, I was still happy to stick with my old "scientific" explanation. I had learned that Judy had enormous difficulty living on her own: she was an extrovert, and extroverts naturally enjoy and feel relaxed in the company of others. But there were added layers to her distress. When she was with others, she could more easily be distracted from her tortured thoughts. Perhaps even more importantly, when she was on her own, she was left with just herself—the person she despised most.

Judy's fear of being alone didn't leave her, and she required several more admissions to hospital, but she survived the remainder of that time alone, during which Stacey had given birth to her second child, Paige. Travis was the father again, but their relationship was rocky and they soon separated. Years later, Judy told me that Travis had spent time in prison after being convicted of assault.

Stacey and Judy needed each other, and Judy soon moved again to be with Stacey and the grandchildren. It worked for a while, and even for some months after Stacey's new boyfriend, Karl, moved in, but eventually her relationship with Stacey and Karl became strained and Judy's immediate solution was to move into the local caravan park. It was now some five years since her attack of Guillain-Barré syndrome and she was back living on her own, leaving me searching for something that would help her and anxious about what might come.

5. Still alive—just

I had heard about Judy's move to the caravan park over the phone, and at our next session she was bubbling over with the frustration of those events. She looked a wreck, though her hair was a wild and vibrant purple, her favourite colour.

"They've kicked me out. She said she'd call the police. How could she? She's so mean, and John, I do so much with the kids. I don't think she'll cope. I actually liked Karl to start with, but he's hopeless. She calls me a drug addict but, honest, she's taking more stuff than me. I really worry about her."

"Judy, you know Stacey; she's very likely to need your help in the future. I know you worry about the kids, but I think you need to let Stacey do her thing. She's probably giving you a hard time because she's scared to be without you."

"Johhnnn." A deep and drawn-out John meant there was significant gravitas attached to her next statement. "I don't trust him."

Judy's need to talk and communicate her fears usually dominated the session, and I frequently felt that my "words of wisdom" weren't heard. So I was often conscious of repeating myself. "Judy, I think it's hard for Stacey to be without you," I reiterated, "and I'm sure she'll need your help in the future, but right now we have to get you looking after yourself. And you're no good to them if you get worse."

"But John..."

And so it went. She was on her own again, and I was worried.

Judy hated Stacey's neighbourhood, where she had been living. Her negativity about it was virtuosic.

"John, there were two drug dealers in our street and another one around the corner, and rubbish everywhere. They just dump stuff, and the houses are all falling apart. No one cares."

The caravan park in that same area was obviously just as bad. I had always been aware that Judy, despite her "rough as guts" demeanour, had a sense of style. One day, she came to her appointment and roundly criticised me for the appearance of the practice's waiting areas. We had recently placed a large plastic plant in one waiting room, and my secretary had distributed many smaller plastic plants and flowers of lesser quality around the public spaces.

"John, you're turning the place into a dosshouse—you've got to get rid of them."

Of course she was right, and they were soon gone.

Around that time, I was having my own health problems. I'd had a melanoma and several basal cell carcinomas excised from my very Celtic skin. I'd also suffered an uncomfortable period of seronegative arthritis, from which I recovered, and more recently a couple of attacks of iritis (inflammation of part of the eye). In years to come, I would see those ailments as a corollary of the lack of balance in my life. Right then, I was in the process of having a large area of solar keratosis on my right cheek burnt off with cream. It looked pretty awful, and that day, before I could explain my appearance, Judy said, "Jesus, have you got the Jack Dancer?"

It took me a few seconds to work out what the Jack Dancer was as I crossed my legs somewhat defensively, not wanting to reveal too much about my own problems. In truth, I feared that it could be precancerous.

"No, I don't have cancer. I have to put a cream on this bad patch of skin to burn it off so it doesn't become a cancer."

"John, if you do go to the Box Condo before me, I'd like that one." She pointed to a painting on the wall of my room depicting the rooftops of Richmond.

"And if you croak, they should just put you in a freezer and I could come and have my sessions as usual. I reckon that would work. I'd know what you would say. You're the Big-Picture Projectionist. I bring in all the problems and you give me the big picture. I reckon it would work. And don't forget, I want that painting."

If I died and went to the Box Condo first, I think Judy would have demanded possession of the whole room, including me in the freezer.

Judy's time in the caravan park near Stacey was very brief, and her next move was to a caravan park in the suburb where she had lived when I first met her. This meant she was back seeing her local doctor, James. I knew James would not have necessarily relished the return of Judy with her multitudinous problems; in fact, he had once written to me describing Judy as his most difficult management problem. I also knew he would not refuse to see her again, as he too had a fondness for her. Moving back also meant Judy could reconnect with the social services in the area and be close to her old friends. She wasn't necessarily pleased with the move, but to me it felt like a positive.

Judy spent over a year in that next caravan park, during which time she remained very unwell and required a further admission to a psychiatric hospital in the city. There was no ECT this time, just a period of containment. She eventually moved into her own government-funded house where she remained over the next four years. Three of those were to be spent looking after Dylan and Paige full-time. She was certainly looking after "the kids," as her gold light had suggested she would. This was a connection I was still yet to make. Stacey would visit, but was having her own adventures and eventually her third child Tiana.

Over that five years, there were times when I was scared she would take another massive overdose. After one minor overdose, which she slept off, Judy said, "I knew it wouldn't kill me; it was only sixty tablets. John, I could take Slade's Pharmacy [a large pharmacy near my rooms] and it wouldn't do the job."

I was perversely pleased with that response, as perhaps that meant she wouldn't try again, though I was aware of people who had died taking a minor overdose.

One factor that sustained Judy was her concern for Stacey and now the two older grandchildren. When she was looking after Dylan and Paige, I was impressed with her resilience. I saw Judy with one or both of the grandchildren on a number of occasions. Her commitment to and love for them was obvious, but they also had their problems. Little Paige, in particular, was a very active little girl.

At one of our sessions, Judy vividly described the mess that Paige could create.

"John, she got up in the middle of the night and pulled everything out of every drawer and left it on the floor. I couldn't believe it. I said, 'Al-Qaeda's been at it again,' and you know what she said? She said, 'But Nanna, I thought I was bin Laden.'"

It made me consider whether Paige might have ADHD (attention deficit hyperactivity disorder) though she was still too young to make that diagnosis. Not long after that, I finally acknowledged that Judy herself had ADHD and started treating her for it. It had been easy to avoid, because of Judy's myriad other psychiatric problems. In Melbourne, where I worked, the psychiatric establishment had been slow to accept the idea of ADHD in adults, but Judy's talkativeness, restlessness, distractibility, and impulsiveness all left little doubt. The treatment helped, but as with all her treatments up to then, it was no panacea.

"John, it's good now: there's only three television stations going in my head instead of five," she said.

♦

Closely associated with Judy's fear of being alone was her fear of loss. If a close friend or relative died, she would become frantic. When her friends Padrina and Madrina, who had looked after her when Jonesy was abusive, died within a month of each other, she was inconsolable. When she received letters announcing the death of another old friend, she was distraught, and then again when she also lost a number of close younger friends. At times, she couldn't bear the pain, and discovered that burning herself at least temporarily relieved it.

"I just had to," she would tell me. "It's like there's a voice in my head telling me I have to do it."

"So how do you do it?"

"I heat up a knife on the stove. John, I just have to do something to stop the thoughts."

On two occasions, Judy created full-thickness burns, which needed to be cut out and sutured. On another occasion, when four people had died within a six-month period, she caused a full-thickness burn so large she needed a skin graft. Judy couldn't control it, and I also felt helpless, though uncomfortably relieved that she had burnt herself rather than killed herself. My counselling for her grief and explaining how her past losses magnified her feelings didn't appear to help. The addition of a tattoo, though, was the one thing that did. Having the memory of a person attached to her body gave her comfort.

◆

I had always wondered why Judy didn't have a pet for some company. Once she was back in a house in her familiar suburb, my questioning about this was soon answered.

"John, I need you to sign this form," she said at the start of our session. "It's to say that you think I'm fit to own a snake."

"A snake?" I asked incredulously. "Really?"

"Yeah, it won't be poisonous. John, I love snakes."

"Where would you keep it?"

"You get special homes, like big tanks, and you feed them pinkies— little mice."

"Really?" My verbal skills had left me.

"Yeah, you buy them frozen."

"What do I have to sign?"

"You know, it's a government thing, to say that I'm not mental."

I duly signed and Judy purchased her snake.

At her next session, she asked, "Guess what I called the snake?"

"No idea."

"I've named it JW!"

I had to laugh. "Well, you had better look after it."

Freud would have had a field day with this story, but look after it she did. Several sessions after buying the snake, Judy came to the session with her newly acquired hand-me-down mobile phone. She was struggling with the technology but eventually found a photograph of JW and showed it to me.

"Check him out: he's smiling."

The only smile I could see was the wonderful grin on Judy's face.

"Sure," I replied, lost for words yet again.

"No, seriously, look closer: he's smiling."

Sometimes Judy gave me a gift of the skin JW shed twice a year, and I learned that as it grew, the pinkies had to get bigger and then finally be replaced by frozen rats.

"You put the rat in boiling water to defrost it and soften it."

Judy was certainly part of my ongoing education.

◆

There were, of course, numerous other events and variables that wove into the tapestry of that second decade of my consultations with Judy. She tried two more intimate relationships. The first was with Simon, during the time she was struggling with heroin. It lasted about twelve months.

"I think I was rebelling," she said some years later. "I thought he was pretty cool, you know, leather jacket and motorbike and helmet. He thought he was pretty cool too. He even wanted to marry me. But John, I realised there was nothing there, nothing to him. It was all image."

I enjoyed it when Judy revealed these insights, even if it was some time after the event.

"We sort of stayed friends," she added, "and I did like riding on that bike."

The other sexual relationship was with Peta, and they remained involved for about five years but never lived together.

"She's a girl, John, a woman," Judy somewhat belatedly informed me. I presumed she was concerned I would judge her.

"Well, I'm not that surprised," I said. "In fact, it makes sense, given what men have done to you."

"John, her upbringing was as bad as mine. Seriously, I didn't think that was possible. She hasn't hurt me. She's not like that. But you know what she used to do?" Judy was now almost whispering. "She ran a brothel in Melbourne and she used to administer pain to men and get paid for it. Never had sex with them; that wasn't the deal. She couldn't—she said she could never have sex with a man."

"I'm not surprised," I responded. "Did you know that a large percentage of women in the sex industry have a history of abuse?"

"John, that doesn't make sense."

"I think it's partly to do with getting some sort of control over men and sex. And maybe something to do with thinking that is all they are worth, or all they deserve."

Unusually, Judy was silent for a moment.

"There's something I've never told you. After Dad died and when the funeral was over I had no way of getting home and no money. I asked my uncle, the mean one who abused me, for a lift home. You know what he said? 'NR, NR … No Root, No Ride.' John, I let him have sex with me. I became that little girl again."

Judy was crying now.

"I was so sad to lose Dad, I thought it might give me comfort. After that, I hated myself so much, I couldn't have despised myself more."

At times like this, it was hard to find the right words. I could feel her profound sadness. I couldn't think of another patient who had as much self-loathing.

"I'm glad you told me. It's easy to understand. You were desperately sad and just looking for some affection. In this job, I hear about people doing that sort of thing all the time … and then hating themselves. So now you have to be kind to that little girl and kind to yourself. Let's see if we can look after you both."

◆

The other major factor affecting Judy's progress was her physical health. Her back had always been bad, but worsened after the Guillain-Barré syndrome. X-rays and scans showed a badly damaged lower spine and stenosis of the spinal canal. Her doctors struggled to limit her pain medications, but she often required a morphine patch or opiate medication in some form. I had been pleased when she returned to her old neighbourhood, where James would admit her briefly if she had fallen or was in more pain. Judy had recently been admitted following one such fall, in which she fractured her left upper arm.

She saw me soon after, still using a walking stick that was now a permanent fixture, with her arm in a sling and somehow a bag hung over her shoulder and around her neck. It was summer, so her black hair was shaved on one side and longer on the other. She came into my office and put a muffin on the small wooden chest next to my chair.

"Apple and cinnamon," she said, "Shorty said that's what you usually have."

Judy was on a first-name basis with most of the staff at the Short Black, where I got my coffee.

"Thank you. Shorty knows me well," I said.

"Yeah, better than that nurse at the hospital. John, she's a real cunt."

"Judy, who are you talking about?"

"The night nurse at the hospital. She treats me like a drug addict, like I'm scum."

"Hey, slow down, and tell me what happened."

"I fell again and landed right on the arm. Apparently it's broken at the top, but you can't put a plaster on it. James put me in hospital."

"How did you fall?"

"You know, the pain hits me and my legs just go from under me, and James won't give me morphine and just puts me on all that other stuff. It helps a bit, but not that much. He does let me have extra Valium, and that helps. But that bitch of a night nurse, she's been there too long and thinks she knows everything. The pain was still bad, so I asked for another Panadeine Forte, and she just smiles and tells me to wait another five minutes. She loves it. Man, if I could have five minutes alone with her..." Judy said, growling.

The irony of Judy's statement was that I had never known her to be violent towards anyone but herself.

"She treats me like an addict. She's a cunt."

"I'm not saying she's justified in treating you like that, and I know some nurses love the power, but you do still use heroin sometimes," I offered somewhat punitively.

"God, I hate it when you say that. I know I do, but you make me feel dirty," Judy said, almost in tears.

I was writing a note about her fractured arm when she added, "Don't forget to add 'loser' as well."

"Would you rather I didn't tell the truth?" I said, still feeling a little self-righteous. I had been frustrated by a few difficult patients that morning.

"And now I really feel like scum. I use it for the pain."

"And to escape how you are feeling?"

"Sure, it's the only thing that gives me peace sometimes."

Judy denied ever falling deliberately, though years later she would admit that she quite liked it when she fell. Admission to the local hospital meant a bit of extra medication and time out. Those brief admissions worked as a circuit breaker when her distress was escalating, and I thought they were important.

"So how long did James keep you in hospital?" I asked.

"The next day, I discharged myself. I couldn't stand another night with that cunt, and I found out she was going to be on duty again."

"How long does the sling stay on?"

"Six weeks, but it's okay to move it a bit," she said as she tentatively raised the injured arm.

Later in that session, the other component of her physical health came up.

"And John, James wants me to have one of those tests, you know, a smear. I can't do it. I hate it."

When Judy had her endometrial ablation some twenty years ago, a cone biopsy of her cervix had also been performed. This involved removal of part of the cervix because of cervical dysplasia. She had since had further areas excised or removed because of abnormal cells. Everything about the process repelled her, and she'd been avoiding it for years.

"It's filth, anything there, I just can't, it's filth. If he finds something, then there's more … fuck … then they put you in stirrups."

By then, my own mood was settling, and I had been quietly amused by Judy's uncompromising description of the nurse. I had chosen not to suggest she was projecting her own self-loathing onto the nurse, and also knew this was a painfully sensitive topic that needed to be tackled.

"But it's worse if you put it off: then it's on your mind all the time. You're better off getting it over and done with. I know you hate it. Hopefully it will be fine. Do you trust James?"

"Yes, but it's filth."

It made sense, given Judy's past abuse, that she hated anything to do with that part of her body. In a sense, it had been the source of all her suffering. Yes, she could overcome that when it came to her need for intimacy and love, but deep down it was still "filth."

Several sessions later, Judy, now without her sling, declared that the results of the smear had been normal.

"James said its okay but he needs to check it each year. That's too soon. John, it's still filth."

◆

More than ten years had passed since I had first seen Judy after her Guillain-Barré syndrome. Over that second decade of treatment, she had been admitted to psychiatric hospitals nine times and received three courses of ECT in public hospitals. I was still treating her with high doses of several psychiatric medications, and there were very few that I or others had not tried. Her accumulated diagnoses would have included major depression, conversion disorder, generalised anxiety disorder, agoraphobia, drug abuse, anorexia nervosa, chronic pain disorder, and ADHD. From my perspective, the most accurate overriding diagnoses were borderline personality disorder and chronic complex post-traumatic stress disorder. It was the severity of her childhood abuse, and the associated neglect, that remained the unresolved source of her distress, self-harm, and risk of suicide.

Judy hadn't lost her sense of humour or any of her colour. By luck more than good management, she was still alive, yet she also remained enormously vulnerable. Despite some periods of burnout, I remained very fond of her, but also very aware that my therapeutic endeavours, and those of her other doctors, had not given her any sustained well-being or peace of mind.

At about this time in my own life, far-reaching changes were occurring that would add an entirely new dimension to her treatment.

John's story

6. A world away

"I have a message for a man sitting with the woman. This is a turning point for you, your future is completely different. Keep going; learn as much as you can. Have confidence in yourself, connect with inside, look at your patients, and do not judge. Do not be concerned whether they are old or new souls, or what they're doing, as many people write in your time. People seem old and new because of the illusion of the time sequence. It means nothing. It only means something in your world. Each person that comes to you needs their multidimensional look at life, to understand they're multidimensional. You'll just know who they are because more and more are going to come to you now, learn from others the world's ready for this now. The others' way, the old way, will stifle you—you need to spread your wings. It's an exciting decade coming up for you, and you're learning much.

"…You agreed to do this before you came to the present lives you are in or you think you are in. You are getting new guides in the next few months. These new guides will come in because you are expanding your world. You are expanding your way of practising psychiatry, which is a very valuable, valuable healing road for a world that has a lot of depression."

It wouldn't be long before these words were spoken to me from a spirit realm that, until now, I had refused to consider.

◆

Towards the end of those twenty years of treating Judy, my eldest daughter Margot and her husband Sam said they had to see me. About a year earlier, Sam's brother, Christian, had died from a highly malignant brain tumour. I knew Sam had been very distressed by his brother's death, and he remained in a dilemma about what to do with an old car his brother had left him. The car was a bomb and couldn't be repaired; it needed to go to the wreckers, but Sam felt obliged to keep it.

Margot started the conversation by saying, "Dad, I know you are going to think this is nuts, but we have to tell you. Sam's mum suggested he go and see a medium. Her name's Monica. She thought it might help with his feelings about Christian. You know Sam's mum is into that stuff, and apparently she's very good. So Sam rang up and made an appointment anonymously so she had no idea who he was. Anyway, I'll let Sam tell you what happened."

Sam went on to describe events with Monica.

"She said that the dead people communicate with her and then try to provide evidence that it's them. She then described a guy who was a young man who was pleased to say 'g'day'."

Nothing too specific about that, I thought.

"Then she said that he was talking about a car and that the car is connected to him and that I should do what I like with it, and apparently he said to not be sad for him and to get rid of the car."

I had to admit that was pretty specific.

"At some stage, she said that the young man was using the word 'Timmy' and that he was laughing," Sam explained. "When I was a teenager, Christian and my other brother used to tease me and call me 'little Timmy'."

Okay, so that's also pretty specific, I thought.

"And here's why we had to tell you: Monica then said that Christian reluctantly stepped aside because someone wanted to say hello to *John*, because he knew he wouldn't get another opportunity. Apparently she could see someone in a uniform and he looked very dapper."

I had to admit it sounded rather extraordinary. My father, who had been in the navy and was always well groomed, had died a few years earlier. If that was my father, he was right about not getting an opportunity to say hello. Neither I nor my siblings were about to visit a medium, though my brother was surprisingly curious about a ghost in the cottage he owned in France.

Margot and Sam gave me a copy of the taped recording of Sam's session with Monica, and it was exactly as they had described.

Not long after she and Sam told me about the medium, Margot visited Kate and me at home. The usual hugs and catch-ups dispensed with, Margot raised the purpose of her visit, again hesitantly.

"Dad, you know how I am thinking of writing a young-adult-fiction book? I think I might use reincarnation as one of the themes."

A good device to create some drama, I thought, but said nothing.

"Well, I've read this book by a psychiatrist called Brian Weiss. It's called *Many Lives, Many Masters*. I think it's very interesting, and I'd really like your opinion. Here—I've brought you a copy."

I had always been a slow reader, and had enough reading material on my list to sink a ship, but knew Margot would not ask if it was not important. Kate and I were also about to embark on a resort holiday in Thailand, which I knew would give me the perfect opportunity to read. So I agreed, and the rest, as they say, is history.

In a beautiful seaside environment near Phuket, the book practically jumped into me. I read it in one day—a record for me. At the time, I couldn't explain why I felt so positively and strongly about what Dr Weiss had written. It was compelling; I knew I could not ignore it. Here was a respected psychiatrist, internationally published, with a strong academic and clinical background, whose patient had inadvertently, under hypnosis, described her memories of a past life centuries ago. That patient then went on to describe extraordinary details about Dr Weiss and his family that she could not possibly have known.

Kate also read the book in just an afternoon, and when I asked what she thought, to my delight she said, "It just makes sense. As I was reading it, I kept wanting to say, 'It all fits'." When we returned home to Melbourne, I told my daughter I loved it, and excitedly she exclaimed, "Oh, thank God. I was really nervous about asking you. I thought you'd think I was loopy."

I ruminated on the issues raised by the book for some months to come. I couldn't let it go, yet at the same time it challenged the foundations of how I saw myself. I was in an odd state of excitement and confusion, knowing that my life was irresistibly changing.

◆

During the year that followed reading *Many Lives, Many Masters*, I felt like I was being besieged by events that reinforced the importance of my new way of thinking. It was new for me, but I was discovering it was hardly new for others, even within the scientific community.

Not long after our trip to Phuket, Kate and I moved into a new home. Our neighbours invited us over for coffee, and the first words Michael, a retired pharmacist, said to me were, "What do you think about hypnosis?" Michael, who knew I was a psychiatrist, went on to describe having witnessed hypnosis being used in a group setting. One man in particular, he said, went back to the memory of his very difficult birth, and at the end of the regression had a distinct red mark around his neck. His birth had apparently been complicated by the cord being wrapped around his neck. When I was obviously interested in his story, Michael then went on to tell me about his own near-death experience when he had almost drowned during his childhood.

I was becoming much more willing to talk about mystical matters with my patients. A good example was Deborah, a very capable woman who suffered bouts of depression and had for a long time felt she had psychic abilities. We discussed this during her session, and she was pleased that I was more receptive to such phenomena. At the end of the session, as she was walking out, she turned to me and asked, "So, how are your feet? I don't mean to intrude, but it's just come to me that you have had problems with your feet." Deborah couldn't have known about the episode of arthritis from which I was now recovered, nor that it had particularly affected my feet.

I decided to keep a journal of these stories, because I knew that over time I would otherwise rationalise them as insignificant or simply forget. My reading habits changed completely. Not only was I reading more, but nearly all the material was related to reincarnation and psychic or spiritual phenomenon. I also returned to some of my old hypnosis texts. During my final year of psychiatric training, I had been involved in a course run by the Victorian Hypnosis Society, during which I learned hypnosis skills. Though I had only used hypnosis occasionally in my practice, I considered myself lucky to have this skill, as it was not normally part of psychiatric teaching. I know now that my exposure to the hypnosis course was no coincidence. I pulled out my old books and bought some new ones to reacquaint myself.

Kate had loved *Many Lives, Many Masters*; she had a much more religiously involved upbringing than I had, but while not atheist, was disillusioned with the rigidity and inherent rules of religious institutions. For her, the Church's loving tenets were lost amid the rules and regulations and inevitable human power struggles. Kate had been discussing the book with her friends, and an old friend, Jenny, showed particular interest, as she had always had a fascination with spiritual matters. She had done a lot of reading in this area and considered it very likely that she had past lives.

Their discussions led to Jenny offering herself as a guinea pig if I wanted to trial my hypnotic regression techniques. When Kate told me, I was immediately both eager and anxious, but I knew there was no significant risk and felt compelled to take up Jenny's offer.

Jenny's story

7. Always meant to be

> Reincarnation, whatever that is, is more likely than not because we are here.
>
> *Antoni—my patient*

◆

Jenny was slightly older than me, with a lovely, youthful nature, and was married with three adult children. She openly admitted to having a few insecurities, but had never needed a psychiatrist. Her anxieties, she said, were prone to cause tummy problems, something similar to irritable bowel syndrome. As a young girl, she had an innate interest in the mystical, but her curiosity had been belittled by some of her family and she had learned to hide it.

Armed with my newly memorised induction techniques, including a lot of Brian Weiss's methods, I arranged to see Jenny in my rooms after my last patient one day. At that stage, I didn't have a couch or recliner chair, so she sat in the usual consulting chair opposite me. Jenny admitted to being quite anxious, as I was, though I didn't declare it. To my enormous relief, she was a wonderful hypnotic subject. I wanted to believe it was my fabulous technique, but I suspect I could have bungled it and she still would have gone into a highly focused state. As part of my deepening routine, I had asked Jenny to imagine herself in a garden, and she later told me that in the garden she was met by her deceased father, who had reassured her and said, "Listen to the voice and what you will learn will be good for you."

Initially, Jenny went into a thirteenth-century French life as a young male working on a farm. He had a sore back but had to help the workers with the hay because they needed to get it in before the weather changed. His father owned the farm and had taught him to treat the workers well.

Annoyingly, I had forgotten to bring a voice recorder and was madly taking notes. Captivated by what was unfolding in front of me, I don't think I blinked once during the whole session. Fortunately, Jenny was speaking quite slowly and often repeating herself, so I was able to take some detailed notes. Some of her dialogue went as follows:

"The job (gathering the hay) is done and everyone is really pleased. I am sixteen but quite strong physically. There is laughter in the group. Mum tells me not to get drunk, as if I would. (Laughs.) How does she know I've had a drink? She is overprotective, short, and dumpy. Father is a good man. He taught me to be good to co-workers. Someone brings up the English; the family talks about them as being a nuisance. 'Why don't they stay on their little island?' My uncle says they have two heads. (Laughs.) I have never met one, though."

Jenny's descriptions were detailed, and I was somewhat mesmerised. The young man whose life she was remembering—I forgot to ask his name—went on to marry a girl who was half English. He had been slow to marry because they were fighting a war against the Italians. When I took Jenny forward in that lifetime, she found the man in chains in a dungeon, having been captured during the war. Starving, and so thin he felt he could almost slide out of the chains, he worried about his wife and daughter and wished it were all over. He eventually died in the dungeon and floated out of his body and then above the castle where he'd been held captive. He felt completely calm. In that spirit state, he soon encountered his father and mother, who were "loving and so pleased to see me." He was told that he had done well and fulfilled the purpose or learned the lessons of that life. He had "learned to treat women well."

I was entranced by Jenny's description of the afterlife.

"We don't talk: we communicate easily by telepathy," she said. "My guide is helping me to assimilate back into the spirit world, because I am still worried about my wife and child. I am being taken to a library with lots of books, going forever. I am shown a book and can read the writing. It's not English, but I now know my wife and daughter are fine. Then I'm taken to a healing room. It's wonderful and calm, and I can feel all the elements of my soul coming together—an odd sensation. I'd like to stay here for a while. Later, I will talk to my guides or teachers."

Her guides had already told her that she still had chains or restraints around her and that she needed to break free, to trust and believe in herself.

After I had been writing for a minute or so in silence, and without my prompting, Jenny explained that she had chosen another life, and said, "I don't want to go into the womb too soon, because it can be boring." She said, "It will be a brief life but an important lesson. The masters are worried though, that it might leave an *imprint...*"

I still hadn't blinked when Jenny went on to explain that she was squeezing into a fetus. In my mind's eye, I was trying to imagine how Jenny's spirit might achieve this, but that was for later.

She then described being born in Africa, where her mother cut the umbilical cord and left her under a tree because she was a girl and not a boy. The mother didn't come back, and Jenny detailed feeling hungry, alone, and abandoned, starving and crying. Finally she said, "It's raining. I've stopped crying and the rain is crying for me." She then left that body and said, "I have learned to understand what it's like to be abandoned, because I abandoned a child in a previous life."

Sweet Jesus, I thought to myself as I brought Jenny out of her deep trance, if it hasn't left an imprint on her, it's certainly going to leave one on me. Jenny took a while to reorient herself, but after a brief walk around the office and a glass of water she was fully grounded and back in the room. She was amazed, and said she had never expected the experience to be so dramatic and detailed.

Jenny had a clear memory of the lifetimes she had described, and was able to recount some additional details. She felt that her father in the French life was also her father in this life, and that her mother in the French life was her paternal grandmother in this life. From my reading, I had already become aware that souls or soul groups reincarnated together but often with changed roles. She said that although they looked completely different, it wasn't hard to identify who they were in this life. Jenny also felt that the lessons of each life made sense to her, and admitted that she had always held a fear of abandonment in her current life. The detail that most amused me was her marvelling at how physically strong she felt in that French life.

"Is that how you guys feel? It was so strange. Man, it felt good."

Jenny and I were both delighted by the outcome of the regression, and we agreed to meet again. In fact, we ended up completing five more sessions. I recorded the remaining five, and in each one she went into an exceptionally deep and focused state. She experienced a further ten lives spanning time and cultures, male and female, sometimes dying young and sometimes living to an old age. They included lives in ancient Egypt, soldiering in the war between Athens and Sparta, as an indigenous person in Tahiti and a merchant in China, Elizabethan England, Alabama during the American Civil War, and more. I was struck by how spontaneous Jenny became and how completely embedded she was in the feelings, observations, and events of each life she had experienced. There was no sense that it was imagined or contrived. Jenny didn't go back to any famous or infamous lives. Perhaps the closest contact with "famous" was her life as Lizzie.

"How old are you, do you think?"

"Seven."

"Are you a boy or are you…?"

"I'm a girl. I'm a girl. I know I'm plain, but you can tell I'm a girl."

"Have a look around. Are you inside or outside?"

After Jenny's first session, I had made a mental list of orienting questions to ask during future regressions.

"I'm in my mum's bedroom. In my mother's bedroom. She's frantically fiddling around and the maids can't seem to satisfy her. My mother's stunningly beautiful. She's taking this dress off and they're putting that dress on and her headdress is wrong. I sit there and I think, 'I know exactly what would work for you, Mother'."

"Is there anyone else there?"

"There are two ladies. They're her maids. One gets frustrated; she just adores my mother. The other just goes along with it. I don't know how she thinks. She's got no time for me; she doesn't like me. So I just keep out of her way, 'cause when my mother's not looking, she'll give me a bit of a nudge."

A slight pout appeared on Jenny's face as she spoke of the "nudge."

"Are there any other children around?"

"No."

"Are you the only child, do you think?"

"No, I have two big brothers."

"Do you know what your name is?"

"Lizzie."

"And do you know what the date is?"

"1559."

Occasionally, there was a pause before Jenny answered questions, but her complete enmeshment in the memory usually resulted in a quick answer.

"And where are you? Do you know the country?"

"London. We're in London in one of the new queen's big homes, well, palaces. I never see the new queen. She's got red hair like me, but my mother says she's much prettier than I am. Mother's one of her ladies in waiting."

"And who's the queen? Who's the new queen?"

"Queen Elizabeth."

I took Jenny forward in time, and at age thirty, Lizzie had been married for eighteen months and was now pregnant. "My mother said when you're plain, you're lucky to get married, so I felt lucky when I was getting married. But I'd rather do my drawings … I'm very pregnant and I'm really afraid … don't feel well."

"Take yourself forward now to the delivery, to the labour," I said.

"Very cold," she whispered. "I feel cold." She shivered and exhaled. "I'm very cold."

"If it's distressing, just allow yourself to float above it."

"Freezing. Baby's come out. Baby's come out—it's a boy. Oh. I've done my duty as a wife. So cold." She shivered, and her breathing was laboured. "Someone's saying, 'Don't forget the mother. Look after the mother.' I'm so cold. I'm getting weaker and weaker."

"Do people around notice?" I asked, as I was starting to get caught up in the anxiety of the moment. The emotions and feelings Jenny was describing were palpable.

"Yes, they're starting to panic. I hear someone…"

"My mother's saying, 'She's losing too much blood.' I've never seen my mother look so upset. She looks distressed. My mother's starting to look old. Mother's starting to look old." She shivered again. "It's so cold," she whispered.

"Do you survive this?"

"There's a light at the end of the room." Her voice was still very faint.

"You can see a light?"

Jenny was then silent for a while. As I heard a car revving in the street outside, I realised that I had almost been in a trance myself. With a deep breath, Jenny then spoke again.

"I'm out of the body."

"What do you see and what do you feel?"

After a brief pause, Jenny continued.

"I see stars, lots of sparkly stars. I'm still cold. And I'm on a mountain and there's snow, lots of snow." She took a deep breath. "So cold." Another deep breath. "I can hear dogs barking, and it's cold and cold."

Jenny had gone straight from the end of her life as Lizzie into another life. Perhaps it was that feeling of being cold that had triggered a memory of another time when she had been so cold.

"How old are you now?"

"Forty. Nearly forty-one."

"Do you know your name?"

"Can't say it. I know what it is… I can't say it. It's … can't get my tongue around it."

I could see the frustration on Jenny's face. I would have loved her to start speaking in an unknown foreign language, as some people had done in past-life regressions. Sadly, that didn't happen.

"Is it a foreign name … an unusual name?"

"Yes."

"What country do you live in?"

"I think its China."

"What are you wearing?"

"Fur skins. I've got a fur hat on. I'm on the border of China and Russia."

I was contemplating the geography as Jenny took another deep breath.

"Are you male or female?"

"I'm a man."

"And you're outside? Or inside?"

"Outside. It's starting to snow again. We're not going to make it. Not going to make it to the next town. It's getting bad, worse and worse." She was shivering and breathing deeply again as she told this story.

"Who are you with?"

"Couple of other men."

It was disconcerting for me to see Jenny actually shiver while reliving that life. I had made sure my consulting room was warm before the session, as I knew that being in a trance state for an extended period could leave you feeling cold. The room temperature was clearly not the problem.

"Is there anyone around that you know from this lifetime?"

"One of them is my brother. I don't know the other."

"Do you know what you've been doing?"

"We've been trekking. Travelling. We're travellers. We're merchants. Our sleighs are full of merchandise—silk. But we've made a mistake, the, the one of the men [sic], wanted to go, and I thought, 'No, we should wait.' I had a feeling the weather's going to turn. Sssso much snow."

"And are you walking through the snow?"

"We can't, we've stopped, we're trying to … it's getting colder and colder and colder and it's just not…" Jenny was now breathing deeply and exhaling audibly while explaining events.

"Do you know what time it is? What date it is?"

"It's very ancient times? It's BC."

"Are you worried you're going to die there?"

My emotions had got the better of me again. The question was obviously rhetorical.

"I've gone. Oh, that's warmer." She inhaled deeply. "Ah … travelling through light. Back into the garden … I'm in my garden."

On most occasions after death, Jenny would give vivid accounts of her experiences between lives in the spirit world. I occasionally glanced at the digital recorder working away on the little table next to her. I was so pleased to have recordings, because there was an enormous amount of new information to digest.

"I am resting now. I am just being."

"Can you describe how that feeling is?"

"I am everything and I am all things and I am me and I am everything. There's nothing really more to say. It just is."

At that point, Jenny's phone rang loudly, startling me but not her.

"Ignore that ringing," I said. "Just be there in that moment, in that state. Have you chosen the next physical form you're going into?"

"Not yet. I am staying here for a while. I am busy with creation."

"Can you describe to me what you mean by creation?"

"Just creating with my thoughts. Creating geometry … all of us … all live beings. Because I like doing geometry. I love it, I love it."

I wasn't sure what "geometry" meant in that spirit state, but I was going with it.

"Are there others doing the same thing?"

"Oh yes. I can feel everyone around me. They're part of me and I'm part of them. So blissful."

"What are you creating?"

"Expansion. Oh, I keep seeing Earth. It looks like there's a … down there … Oh, there is. There are beings asking for help with Earth. It's… such a tiny little speck in that, that perceived universe. But it is mis-creating, it needs people, needs people to incarnate to help. Needs light. There are beings of light on the planet and they've forgotten who they are. How could they… ah, ah …" She sighed.

I couldn't think of a time when beings on Earth hadn't been mis-creating and needing help, but for me, Jenny's most poignant comment was that we had forgotten who we are. Her insights from the spirit state were often completely unexpected, and they continued.

"And does it feel good in the spirit world?"

"Oh yes! Yes. And you think to yourself every time you come back, you think, 'Why do I leave here?' I must be insane, but to remember completely who I am I have to get … it's like karma, some religions call it karma … deal with the karma finally. You just have to let it all go, because I've forgotten this last life now. When was it? Oh yes, that's right, because it's an illusion, it's not real, and the next one will feel real, but they're not really real."

I think even Jenny, while remembering her time in that spirit state, had trouble finding the words to describe the knowledge she had in that form. I asked her: "What's real … is the spirit?"

"Mm, mm, the spirits are there to call on, but human beings have got amnesia. But that's for a purpose, because to do what they need to do on Earth. If they remembered everything, they'd be distracted. But they have guides; they've got points of attraction; they've got people they're meant to meet. But there's no right or wrong here. It just is. It's what you choose."

"There's no judgement?"

"No. The judgement is misunderstood on Earth. We judge ourselves, and we are our harshest critics, and we project our misery onto other people instead of going within."

I was surprised by the sophistication of some of Jenny's comments. In psychiatry, we understand how easy it is to deny our own feelings and project those feelings onto others. At the end of the session, I was pooped. My brain was overflowing with ideas: telepathy, they're part of me and I'm part of them, mis-creating but no judgements, and last but definitely not least, that our lives feel real but are just illusion. Jenny looked fine but I needed to go home and rest my frontal lobes—real or otherwise.

♦

From what Jenny was saying, I gleaned that there were discussions between souls before choosing each life. After one life and while in the spirit state, she spoke of her deliberations before two brief lives.

"What's happening now?" I asked.

"I've just been asked to help within my group. They've asked me to be a child and die young, so they can learn lessons. Oh, not again. I've done this before. This seems to be my specialty. Okay. Okay, I'll do it."

"Do they ask that of certain souls?"

"Um … everyone takes it in turns and they've helped me out. They'll help me out in the next big long life. They'll help me out if I help them out this time. We're talking about it. It's a big discussion. I think I'll go into … I don't know, I don't know if I'll go there… I will go there. I'll be a boy, okay. A boy in … Czechoslovakia, okay. I'm going to be in an orphanage. That will be very sad."

"Do you choose that life?"

"Okay, I've agreed, I've agreed to … and …"

Jenny jumped straight into her memories of that life.

"I've got striped pyjamas on and it's really dark and horrible. I've got sores all over me. Oh. Starving. Starving, starving, I'm starving. I've moved out. Moved out."

"Out of that life?"

"Yes."

"It sounded difficult."

"It was just very sad. A very sad country at this time."

"And were you abandoned?"

"I don't know what happened to me. I'll go and find out. I'm still that child, and I don't know what happened to me."

On a number of occasions, it was evident that in the spirit state, the soul was given information to help heal any residual fears persisting from the previous life.

"No, my parents were killed in an accident and they were very distressed leaving that life knowing they left me. I died."

"And you died in the orphanage?"

"Yeah. Yeah."

"Have you now moved on from that life?"

"Yes."

"Are you back in the spiritual world?"

I was a bit slow on the uptake that evening.

"Yes. Now there are big plans for a life in the second half of the twentieth century, but there is talk about being a child again and dying as a child again." She sighed. "Don't know if I want to do that. I don't know. I don't know."

I was feeling pretty sure she shouldn't do it, but despite my silent protestations, Jenny then went straight into memories of that life.

"Bombs going off, bombs. Bombs going off all the time, bang. I hate it. I'm blocking my ears. Here they go again, my dad says, "Bloody Germans." They'll never get London. "Bloody Germans," he's saying. Then he goes and fights. Mother sends me out into the country. I don't want to go; I don't want to go."

"How old are you?"

"I think I'm five. I might be nearly five."

"Are you a boy or a girl?"

"I'm a boy. Do I look like a girl?" Jenny was frowning, and gave a groan as she continued. "It's these ugly clothes I have to wear. I'm in clothes too big for me."

"And are you in London or...?"

"Yes. I'm going on a train. Train trip. I don't want to go. My mother is angry because she's coming with me. Other children are going on their own without their parents. I like the hat. I like that hat."

"Do you know what your name is?"

"John."

"Do you have any sisters or brothers?"

"No. Mother's putting her overcoat on me now, so it's really, it's too big. I hate this overcoat. I look stupid in it."

As Jenny frowned again, I was staggered by her total absorption in that memory.

"Are any of the people there? People you know from this lifetime?"

"Mother, it's my cousin Meredith. I know, and I am hurrying. She's saying we're almost late, hurry. My mother's very slim and very quick and she dances a lot. She's a dancer. We're in the train now... off we go. I'm going to drive a train when I grow up, when this dumb old war finishes ... I'm in the light. I'm in the light. Oh this is ... hey, this is cool. They're better clothes. Oh."

"What's happened?"

"It's a train wreck."

"Oh, I'm a bit confused about what's happened. It's a train, ah ... I can see my body."

"Are you looking down on it?"

"Yeah. My hat's fallen off. I've got a big cut on my head that I can see. Poor body. Okay. I'm going. Time to go. Leaving dumb old war anyway... into the light."

"That was a brief life. Were there any lessons from that life?"

"I've got to stop whinging. I whinged a lot in that childhood. I felt overwhelmed by it. My mother was killed too. Poor Father, coming back to..."

"Do you feel safe now?"

"Oh yes. It was the plan. Father had lessons to learn. That's his business, not mine."

"So, that was the plan?"

"That was the plan. Mother and I, we were to go, because we're going to be related in the next life."

What a journey! I felt jubilant and privileged at witnessing Jenny's recall of her past lives. There were many similarities with Catherine's dialogue in *Many Lives, Many Masters*, as well as with other books I was reading. In addition, there was new information I had not yet read about, especially Jenny's depiction of the spirit realm and what happened after death, or for that matter the process of the spirit joining the fetus before birth. We were meeting weekly, so there was a hell of a lot to comprehend and incorporate into my excited mind. And then there was the uncertainty of where all this was going to lead me and possibly even my patients.

8. A message from the masters

> Progress is impossible without change, and those who cannot change their minds cannot change anything.
>
> *George Bernard Shaw*

◆

I was grateful to have a week between regressions with Jenny. I couldn't help but wonder what past lives I might have lived. At one stage, while in the spirit realm, Jenny had been told she had lived 210 lives. Surely that's too many, I thought, but who was I to start applying human logic to something that went well beyond our earthly perspective? Jenny was also embracing her new knowledge, and during the week sometimes found herself flipping back to memories of those past lives. She was always enthusiastic when she arrived the following week.

Until now, Jenny's past lives had been quite dramatic. I was relieved when her next memory was of a long and lovely life in Tahiti, even if her death had been somewhat unusual. Her description of it all started when she was seven, and I asked, "How are you feeling?"

"Very, very happy. It's just fun. We swim and we laugh, we play, we learn to dance, we sing ... I sing a lot ... I like to sing."

"Do you have brothers and sisters?"

"Yes. I have some that are of same parents and I have some I share a mother and I have some I share a father."

"And is that normal?"

"Yeah, I think so. I don't know. It seems to be what everyone does. Is there any other way? I don't know."

I loved it when Jenny was so engaged in the experiences that she lost her sensibilities from this life. She told me her name was Aura, and that during that life she had five children and her passion was making jewellery, but she also made clothes and baskets. I enjoyed listening to the freedoms she recalled from that life and culture. Eventually, I instructed her, "Take yourself forward again, perhaps to the end of that life."

She paused first, and then she said, "I'm walking into the sea. I have said farewell in my mind to everyone. I have walked into the sea. I will not be back. The waves are engulfing me now. They're like cushions. They're like a cloak. The waves are my friends. I have always loved the waves. My heart is weak. I am just laying here and it will just stop. I know."

"Are you alone?"

"Yes. They all know I have chosen this. They know I love the sea. They know I'm choosing to go."

There was no sense that Aura was distressed, and nor were there any signs of concern on Jenny's face. Her chosen means of euthanasia struck me as being a very accepted and peaceful end to that life.

The other long life Jenny lived was as Rosalind in Alabama in the 1800s. At the very start of that life, I asked, "Can you describe to me what's happening?"

"I am laying in my crib. There is sadness around me. My mother has died. I think it's my fault. I think I killed her. She's giving me a kiss and she's going to the light. She's going. She said everything would be okay."

It was common for Jenny's dialogue and insights to have a very playful or almost Pollyanna quality, and yet to have an enlightened perspective as if her soul or spirit was describing events. I wondered if young children saw the world in this uncomplicated and non-critical way.

Rosalind survived the American Civil War as a young woman, but lost her husband in a tree-felling accident at thirty-one. She never really recovered and remained withdrawn and irritable, but despite that went to a few movies in her old age, and I enjoyed her assessment of them.

"That man in that movie looks like my father ... I don't think those movies will go anywhere, those pictures, those tawdry stupid pictures they keep showing."

"How old are you now?"

"I'm sixty-five and I'm dying. I'm glad to die. I saw that movie and he looked like my father. So looked like my father."

"The man in the movie?"

"Yes. But he's … the man in the movie, it's the funeral of Edward VII, you know, the king in Great Britain. He's died, I'm dying with him, we're much the same age. He's a little bit older than me, I think. I don't really know, but it's around about and I'm watching his funeral and I think … good, I'm going, I'm full of arthritis. I'm full of pain."

Later, Jenny and I both laughed at how wrong Rosalind was about the movies going nowhere. Before and after sessions, we would also discuss the impact of the regressions and how the new knowledge related to her current life. Apart from her fears of abandonment, she had also been frustrated by a tendency to be slightly overweight. We wondered whether starving to death in a couple of lifetimes might have contributed to her need to eat more and keep weight on.

In her life as an Athenian soldier, Jenny went straight to the battlefield.

"How old do you think you are?"

"Nineteen."

"And do you know where you are?"

"Between Greece and Greece, that sounds funny, doesn't it, and I'm from Athens."

"Okay, and is it a war?"

"Yes."

"And are there bodies around you?"

"Oh, hundreds … and swords and horses and shields … screaming, the screaming and yelling, but I feel detached. That's why I think I'm dying. I think I'm losing a lot of blood. Oh."

I was getting better at not getting caught up in Jenny's emotions as I asked, "What are you wearing?"

"Just the soldier's uniform. You know the usual."

"Where have you been injured, do you think?"

"I've lost a leg. I think that's what's happened. I don't think my leg's there anymore. I felt a searing pain and I feel weird."

"Do you know what the time is, or the date of that period?"

"It's modern times, you know, Athens versus Spartica."

I had to smile, and I half expected Jenny to do the same with the irony of that statement. She didn't, of course, because she was completely ensconced in the memory of her life as that soldier. His name was Andrononis, and he died on the battlefield and then travelled through a tunnel.

"I feel other people with me. I don't know if they're people, but there are other people there too," she said. And soon after, "People are light and then they're people and then they're sort of turning to light again and then they're people again … that's strange. They're saying, you'll get used to it."

"Is that their way of showing you who they are?"

"Yes, who they were to me in my life. Oh, there's my favourite uncle. He was funny. 'Hello, Uncle.' And there was the commander that died last year. He's waving at me. He was so good to me. He was a soldier, but he was quite the philosopher actually. He was a wise man. He's saying, 'See me later.' I'm just talking to people now."

"And who do you talk to?"

"They're wanting me to go somewhere. People are taking me. One looks like a female. The other two appear to be male, but you really wouldn't say they're male or female. I don't know. It's hard to describe. They're telling me to stop limping. I didn't realise I was limping. They're saying, 'You've got your leg, don't worry about it, the body's gone.' Oh, of course it has. I'm going through … like I'm seeing my life how it was. I had many sisters. I teased them a lot! I can see my favourite, my favourite pet. It's a bird. I thought he was so free, the way he would fly… My sisters felt how lucky I was because I was a boy. I didn't think about it, didn't think of that. That's interesting, there's no hard feelings. Just a little bit of envy."

"So you can see how *they* felt during that lifetime?"

I had read about people having "life reviews" during their near-death experiences.

"Yeah, I can take on everybody else's feelings, thoughts, but not actually thoughts, just a feeling of the thoughts. Seeing the other point of view, if you know what I mean, but there's no judgement, it's just interesting."

Sometimes, when Jenny was in the spirit state, it was hard for me to follow because she was deep in conversation with her guides or other spiritual beings. Upon dying, it was common for her to express the need to orient herself to the spirit state, but without fail she always depicted it as peaceful, restful, or even blissful.

Dr John Webber

In that fifth and second-last session, while in the spirit state after her Athenian life, Jenny received some penetrating insights and advice regarding her current life. We discussed this briefly at the start of her last session, and I reminded her that I would give her a copy of all the recorded sessions. I was also starting to gain confidence with my induction technique, as well as adapting to the variety of circumstances that arose during Jenny's past lives and spiritual experiences. It was our last session, and soon after our discussions, Jenny was back in her usual very deep and focused state.

Initially, Jenny went to a privileged female life in ancient Egypt. I loved her description of learning the healing arts from her mother.

"I am learning all the healing arts. What I'm learning is ointments and creams for various skin problems. My mother is handing down her … she learned it and her mother learned it and now I'm learning."

"And are those ointments applied to…?"

"What they are, they're different ointments and balms and pomanders and all sorts of things. Poultices. They're secrets handed down. It heals all sorts of things, open wounds, red rashes, all sorts of skin outbreaks, ulcers, um … it even has, ointment that helps with lice in the hair."

"So it's an important skill?"

"It is a very important skill. We also learn various cosmetics, and my mother feels I've got my father's gift of invention."

Later, when I asked for the date, she said that it was the twentieth year of the pharaoh's reign. She lived to an old age, and at the end of that life, after she looked down on her pots and jars, there was a long pause. I always got a bit curious during the periods of silence, and this time I asked, "Can you tell me what's happening now?"

"I'm just ready to go, ready for my next life. I think I'll go in the womb now."

"Okay."

"Oh God, it's awful being born. Oh God. Oh dear, my poor mother. Oh, she's not doing too well. My mother's not doing well."

Her mother died, but Toula had a relatively happy life and was trained to be a high priestess. She recalled learning special dances and healing techniques while living in a temple dedicated to the goddess Aphrodite. Again she lived to an old age, and after her death met her childhood friend

Athena, who had also been a friend in this life. After a period of orienting to the spirit world, she explained that she was being counselled about how we learn in the spirit world, and then how we learn in the human body.

"In the body and in that contrasting world ... have you ever been on Earth?... It's a world of contrast ... You have the choice, to choose what you want, but it's not always easy when you are in the drama. You learn quickly on Earth because it's a planet, well, it's becoming a planet, more and more a planet of contrast, apparently."

She continued these discussions with her guides or masters, and then towards the end of the session she said, "People don't realise. A lot of people now on Earth think death's the end. It's the end of the body. I've been there, they're telling me, thinking it's the end."

"Being fearful of death?" I asked.

"Yes. It's an illusion, but it doesn't feel like it when you're in the dying process. I'm remembering many of my lives now ... I'm going into a room with ... red. I'm going into a room with red, red crystals, um ... oh, it's garnet crystal. Garnet and rubies! Oh, I love rubies. Breathing it in." She took deep breaths.

"Do you know what this room is?" I was a bit confused, and it was evident from Jenny's tone and her shifting expression that she was as well.

"Not sure. They're wanting me ... there's something I've got to do. I don't understand this. It's strange. Now I'm being shown in the great huge flames. A life in ... another future life. I don't want to look at this, who cares. I can't understand what you're doing ... I do now ... wait a minute. Oh, I see, I've got to realise that time doesn't exist here the same as on Earth. I'm just giving this woman confidence of a future..."

I presumed that "they" were giving her spirit messages about her future life, in other words, her current life as Jenny.

"...just passing on my confidence. Well, I don't understand ... Oh, I see, I'm passing on the confidence of those lifetimes in Egypt and Greece. I'm passing on the confidence to this woman that is far into the future. From the last life I just had. I can't see her. They're saying I don't need to."

Jenny had remembered those lives where she had been a healer to give her confidence in her current life.

Then it was to be my turn. There was a very long silence, but it was evident that Jenny was still in that very deep state and orienting herself to something. For some reason, I also remained silent. Finally, Jenny spoke. Her manner was very deliberate and her voice seemed deeper. It didn't sound like Jenny, and I realised that this was a message coming from the spirit realm, perhaps from a master, and the message was for me.

"I have a message for a man sitting with the woman. This is a turning point for you. Your future is completely different. Keep going. Learn as much as you can. Have confidence in yourself. Connect with inside. Look at your patients and do not judge. Do not be concerned whether they are old or new souls, or what they're doing, as many people write in your time. People seem old and new because the illusion of the time sequence. It means nothing. It only means something in your world.

"Each person that comes to you needs their multidimensional look at life to understand that they're multidimensional. You'll just know who they are because more and more are going to come to you now. Learn from others; the world's ready for this now. The others' way, the old way, will stifle you. You need to spread your wings. It's an exciting decade coming up for you, and you're learning much.

"You've done a lot for this woman. You've given her a big key to a really great big scary door. She can move on now; she will be fine. She will learn much and pass on much, but she will have peace within. That will be good and she will understand her gift. It isn't a gift; it's just that she's recognised she can do something that everyone can do—they just don't know it. That's the difference. She knows about it, others don't. There's nothing she can do that other humans can't do. They just don't recognise it, especially in your very restrictive Western world. The Western world has to change now, and it has to realise that people are multidimensional. They are not just one life and then dead at the end, because if they believe that, they are not going to grow as humans. They are not going to grow as spirits, and they will end up in mental illness and depression, which will be a big issue for the first half of this twenty-first century. Depression is a real problem for many, particularly men. It seems to be for women, but it is particularly for men. Men must be allowed to be emotional and express it. You will help many men, because men relate better to men.

"Just ask, what is your next step? Just go inside and see yourself being who you want to be. Picture yourself being who you are, who you want to be, what you hope for, and it will come."

Jenny took a deep breath, and I glanced over at the recorder to make sure it was still on.

"Amber is the colour for you. Amber is an unusual stone. Look into it. The lady has a gift of amber, which is unusual for her, and not very pretty for her, but she had faith in listening to us and got something that she didn't quite understand. She will give it and let go. It's none of her business. How you look at the amber and the colour that goes with it is your business."

"Is the amber for the lady or for me?"

"It is for you from the lady. She kept seeing the colour around you right from the start, but she had it wrong. She thought it was citrine. But when she asked, because she has learned to ask now, we told her it was amber, which is one crystal she has not had anything to do with or ever owned. She owns many crystals, but this one she doesn't have, and so it helped to make her realise she does hear us and not her ego, not her personality, conscious self. She's getting better and better at it all the time, and has a great ability to connect with her guides and the angels. This will only get better and better. She'll be fine. She will have peace for the rest of her life in a way she has never, ever experienced in this life, or in many previous, so-called previous lives. She has not been told about her future lives, because it's not appropriate. All these lives were appropriate for what purpose she was doing it for.

"You agreed to do this before you came over to the present lives you are in, or you think you are in. You are getting new guides in the next few months. These new guides will come in because you are expanding your world. You are expanding your way of practising psychiatry, which is a very valuable healing mode for a world that has a lot of depression."

The message continued to flow from Jenny, but I knew it wasn't coming from her. I'm not sure my eyes could have opened any wider, or my eyebrows lifted any higher, as I tried to take it all in.

"You have given her a great gift, as she has given you a great gift, because she has a great ability to go deep into hypnosis and has travelled in a way that not many will travel, perhaps for a while. She is not ill, as many of your patients will be or are, but she has given you a world that gives you something to work from. Just enjoy yourself and relax and enjoy yourself, because everything will come when it is time. Just be cool, as the lady would say, and go with the flow, because everything will be fine and your family will be fine. Just enjoy them all. Do you have any questions for us?"

Oh my God, I was being asked a question by one of the masters, and I was completely unprepared.

"No. That sounds good. I think I understand to continue down this pathway."

"Definitely, because if you do not, you will become very frustrated, and you will become very ill. You must go down this path and you'll have all the help. Just open your mind to it. You have a partner that will support you and a family in general that will support you. You will have no problem, because there is a great call now for you to do the Dr Weiss type of psychiatry but there are things to learn first, and it will just gradually happen."

"So, do I have the courage to do that?"

"Yes."

"And patience?"

"Yes, courage and patience. You have both in abundance; you will have no problems. It will be fine if you just believe in yourself and trust in your inner teacher. Listen to your inner teacher."

"Yes, thank you."

"And it's not only words you'll hear: it's feelings, it might be a book, it might be a lecture, it might be something that falls on your head, it might be something like a movie, or even be something you hear on the radio that gives you ideas. Just keep your mind open and your ears open and your eyes open."

"Yes, thank you."

"Thank you. We will go now. We will leave this woman."

Jenny took another deep breath, and so did I.

"Okay, it's time to come back now," I said. "Are you okay to come back?"

"Yes, I'm ready to come back."

"In a moment I'll count from one to ten. When I get to ten, you'll open your eyes feeling alert, refreshed, and feeling wonderful, knowing that you are a beautiful, eternal being that is always loved and never alone. When you wake, you'll be in full control of your physical and psychological function, and you'll remember everything from this session.

One … two … three … Gradually more awake but still feeling at peace and wonderful … Four … five … More and more awake … Six … seven … eight … Still calm and feeling wonderful but more awake, more aware of this room and the surroundings … Nine, ten."

Jenny took slightly longer to ground herself after that last session. She stood up and had to shake herself a few times before she sat back down and drank the glass of water I'd fetched for her. She could remember all the details of the Egyptian and Greek lives, but when I mentioned the message from the masters, she had no memory of it. She had enjoyed the regressions: for her they had been very affirming and she was already feeling the benefit. We agreed to do more in the future if there was a need. I thanked her not just for the amber, which I now held in my hand, but for the time she had so generously given me.

When Jenny told me she had no memory of the message from the masters, I felt a slight relief, as I was immediately embarrassed and frustrated by my rather inane questions. Hundreds of alternate questions were already pouring into my mind, but when I thought about it a bit more, I concluded that they weren't so dumb. I was going to need patience and courage if I was to incorporate this new understanding into my life and possibly into my practice. For someone previously rooted in mainstream psychiatry, it was going to be a challenge.

I felt inspired, if not a little overwhelmed, but it was clear I needed to stay cool, take my time, and learn more. I had to get my head around a mass of new information: not just that we had past and future lives, but that we had roles in choosing or not choosing them. I knew a lot of people, especially my patients, who would find that notion hard to swallow. Modern concepts of heaven, hell, and karma were certainly being challenged by the message that there was no judgement and no punishment. Topping it off was the idea that these human lives were just an illusion anyway. A whole new world had been opened up to me, yet applying any of this to someone like Judy was the last thing on my mind.

Other people's stories

9. Opening my eyes

> It is almost an absurd prejudice to suppose that existence
> can only be physical. As a matter of fact, the only form
> of existence of which we have immediate knowledge is
> psychic. We might well say, on the contrary, that physical
> existence is a mere inference, since we know of matter
> only in so far as we perceive psychic images mediated by
> the senses.
>
> *Carl Jung*

◆

Before Jenny's last two regressions, I went on a five-day golfing trip with friends. It felt like my beloved golf was getting in the way of my spiritual pursuits ... or maybe not.

I was travelling with two of my psychiatrist friends, Scott and Graeme, and we were based in beautiful Queenstown, New Zealand. We arrived mid-afternoon and played nine holes of golf, then returned to our hotel with a lovely view of a lake in the distance. The next morning, Scott recalled a vivid dream in which he saw himself standing in the hotel room, looking out the window and seeing a huge wall of water more than two stories high coming across the lake towards him. Graeme then declared that he had also had an unusually vivid dream, of trying to put fires out. They weren't typical fires, and they were out of control. I had not dreamt anything. Golf then became the focus, and we headed off to

Jack's Point to play. At the end of the round, as we sat in the golf lounge, we saw television reports that a tsunami had hit Japan the previous night, damaging the Fukushima nuclear reactor, which was now in meltdown and out of control. We silently watched how the events in Japan had unfolded.

From my new perspective, Scott had symbolically dreamt of the tsunami and Graeme of the fires at Fukushima. I cautiously revealed my feelings and then, wide-eyed, I asked for their thoughts. Scott shrugged; to him, beliefs surrounding the spiritual or metaphysical were simply man's need to come to terms with his underlying fear of death. I was the first to admit the idea of life after death was comforting, but that didn't mean it wasn't real. Graeme was initially reserved, but over time became more inclined to accept that their dreams had been connected to the tsunami and weren't just a coincidence. For me, the lesson was that information from beyond our immediate lives could come to us in dreams.

Psychic phenomena were clearly part of what I was discovering, and I was becoming much more willing to discuss all these issues with my patients. In response, they would often become animated by the opportunity to discuss their own personal experiences.

My patient Phillip had somehow got onto the subject of quantum physics, which he liked. This was another area of science that had become impossible for me to avoid. I explained that I had become interested in quantum theory as well as the whole area of consciousness and psychic phenomena, and the possibility of having past lives. Phillip, in his thirties and highly intelligent, went on to say that he didn't have much time for the psychic stuff, but then told me about an experience he could not explain.

"It was a number of years ago," he said, "and I had been going out with Prue for over two years. She had a few issues, but then again so did I. I thought our relationship was progressing pretty well. So, one day, Prue had an appointment in the city and I drove her in. After dropping her off and driving for a couple of blocks, I felt compelled to turn the car around. I can't explain why I did that. I didn't go exactly back to where I dropped her off, and instead drove into a multistorey car park. I have no idea why, and it was even more illogical because I had no way of paying to get out of the car park. Anyway, I drove in and up to the top of the building, got out of the car, and as I was walking from the car, I saw my girlfriend standing on the edge of the building."

The positive end to the story was that Prue did not jump.

"That's extraordinary!" I offered, gobsmacked.

"I know," Phillip replied, "and you know, I've never told anyone. It's a bit too weird."

I had to conclude that Phillip had been psychically connected with Prue's distress and plans, and had physically responded without knowing why. I wondered how often this happened to all of us. I recalled instances of patients talking to me about having to be near their phones because they knew someone important was about to call them.

I had opened a door to a part of my patients' histories that had formerly been closed off by their own inhibitions or, just as likely, my own intransigence. Either way, I was now feeling much more engaged with and sympathetic to their stories. Patients enjoyed talking about their psychic experiences, and I continued to feel bombarded with their stories—my own personal tsunami.

The next wave of information came from Sharyn, an engaging single woman who had suffered from anxiety and occasional panic attacks, and who had been holidaying in Phuket a few years earlier.

"I'd been lying in the sun," she recounted, "and it was pretty warm. When I opened my eyes, there was Aunty Helen. She said hello, and after I'd blinked a couple of times, she just disappeared. I figured I'd been lying in the sun for too long. I had always been fond of Helen, even though she lived in another state, but when I got home a week later, I heard she had died when I was away. And yes, I did the sums, and she had died just prior to me seeing her on the beach."

Sharyn's experience was certainly not the only one I heard about visitations from someone close that had recently died. In addition, two patients also described having a powerful and profound feeling of sadness come over them, one while riding his bike and another while driving in the country, and then soon after hearing of the death of someone close to them. I wondered if driving and riding resulted in each person going into a mild meditative state that allowed them to receive the feelings. In fact, a common feature of these experiences was that they often occurred at night or in quiet moments when the mind wasn't being bombarded by sensory input.

A similar example came from Terry. He had been a patient of mine for years, was now eighty years of age, and suffered from a well-controlled form of bipolar disorder. He was English, and had grown up in a large and poor family. In his teenage years, he had lived with his grandmother. "My father," he explained, "had been permanently in an asylum for many years. One night, I woke up and there was this being standing next to me. I knew it wasn't anyone real, but I was frozen and couldn't speak. What was interesting was that I wasn't scared at all; I just couldn't move. The only thing this being said to me was, "It will happen in the next seven days," and it repeated it several times. Dad died five days later."

Terry had never forgotten that experience, and it had remained a source of comfort through some of the difficult times of his life. Perhaps that is why he received it.

For my patient Rose, the benefit was much more immediate and practical. Now in her seventies, Rose had also been a patient of mine for a number of years. She would remain well for long periods and then return for a burst of therapy if life events overwhelmed her. She had grown up in a very dysfunctional family, which she escaped by getting married. But, as often happens in those cases, her marriage was equally dysfunctional. She finally extracted herself from her abusive first husband and was left alone looking after her three children back when there was no support for single mothers. She worked part-time but was desperately poor.

"One night," she said, "I woke and had five numbers in my head. Maybe it was a dream, I don't know, but they came from somewhere."

Rose put those five numbers on a Tattslotto ticket. The sixth number she chose didn't come up, but she won second division, which was for her a king's ransom, and life-saving.

Rose had also seen a psychic in the past. I was no longer surprised when patients told me they had seen a psychic, but was still surprised, if not delighted, when they told me the juicy bits. In Rose's case, it was very juicy. The psychic told her she could smell corned beef and pig's trotters. Rose was shocked, because that happened to be her deceased father's favourite meal. As Jenny's masters had said, we all have the ability to tap into our multidimensional selves, and these stories were often examples of just that.

There were even stories about animals. Roger had come to see me after having major surgery for a malignant tumour. His mother suffered from severe dementia, and had been bedbound for a long time. He would visit his mother weekly and read to her, even though he presumed she would have no comprehension. The day after one such visit, he told me that his mother had given him a hug as he packed up to leave. He was shocked that she was physically capable of hugging him. I gently suggested she might be saying goodbye, and Roger agreed. His mother died three days later. Inevitably, this prompted a discussion of what consciousness is and the extent to which it is or isn't connected to our physical body. He then went on to tell me an unforgettable story from his youth.

"We lived in Malvern but would sometimes travel up to our farm past Echuca. Our dog Patch would travel in the trailer behind the car. When we got to Echuca, Dad filled the tank and Patch was fine. Somewhere between Echuca and the farm, he came off, but it was night and we didn't realise until we got to the farm. We searched all weekend but couldn't find him. Three months later, Patch turned up at our home in Malvern, over 250 kilometres away. He was emaciated but alive."

I later learned that Larry Dossey, in his book *One Mind*, had written of similar accounts.

If I was completely honest, there was still a small part of me that was sceptical. Was it all just coincidence, fantasy, or contrivance on the part of the storytellers? Surely, modern science could explain this in a more logical way. I had spent my lifetime discounting such phenomena, though it wasn't just about logic and scepticism. I was starting to realise that the whole idea was challenging my ego. My old identity received great confidence and comfort from remaining attached to traditional medicine and science. It would have been much easier to run with the pack. Yet that small, sceptical part of me was getting smaller all the while. I enjoyed the reading of physicist Max Planck's insight that science progresses funeral by funeral.

Despite my doubts, the avalanche of information continued unabated. I started to take notice of people's experiences with mediums. Of course, there were those who felt they had wasted their money, but then there were those like Cynthia, who saw John Edward in 2008 at the Jika International Hotel in Melbourne.

"It was about five months after Daniel died, and I just happened to see the advertisement on the internet and thought, why not? I went on my own. Now, you know that we had been living in Tasmania and that Daniel had a darker side and could be quite belligerent. Well, halfway through the proceedings, John Edward said there was a Daniel coming through and that he didn't particularly like his energy because he was so pushy. He said Daniel wanted to pass on a message to 'Snoopy.' He then went on to say he was sorry I had taken a hit on the house in Tasmania and that he was embarrassed I had heard about the affair he had in his first marriage; that he was sorry his two sons had been difficult but they would now fade out of my life, and that Muggles, our dog, was with him now. It was all perfectly true—Snoopy was my nickname, he had secretly taken out an extra mortgage on the house, his boys were difficult after he died, and one of them told me about his affair. And Muggles died soon after Daniel died."

For Cynthia, the whole experience had been affirming and liberating. The capacity for mediums to accurately tap into that spirit world astounded me. It was a powerful reminder of our connection with those who had died.

During that first year I had started some reading about children who had talked of their past lives. A friend's son had, on a number of occasions, said that, 'my baby is dead.' The child's comment was not connected to anything in the child's present life. In Western society we are pretty quick to dismiss these sorts of comments. Until then, and despite Jenny's remarks, I hadn't given much thought to children and their spiritual connections, but that was now changing.

The stories continued over the coming years. Mary, an occupational therapist, recounted another wonderful story. She had a young son, Alex, who was not yet three years old but quite verbal and inquisitive.

Mary recalled, "Not long ago, when we were having breakfast, I was talking about my father George, who had died before Alex was born. Alex then said, 'Grandpa George is here, Mum.' I tried to remain composed, and asked him where, and he pointed to one of the chairs. I kept my cool and asked him to say hi, and we talked about Grandpa a bit more. A few weeks later, again at breakfast, I couldn't help myself and asked him if Grandpa George was there, and he said, 'Yes, and Uncle Jack is here too.' I was lost for a moment, but then remembered that my husband had a stepbrother named Jack, who lived in Canada. We went to a wedding over there when Alex was only six months old, but I don't think he ever saw his uncle. Jack had been unwell for years, and he suicided five months later. At the time, Michael and I talked about it for a week or so, and Alex may have heard us, but he was barely a year old. Anyway, I asked Alex where Uncle Jack was, and he pointed to the doorway and said, 'He's comfy cosy'."

I'm sure Mary could see the broad smile on my face as she completed the story.

"Later that day, I couldn't help myself and I pulled out the family photos. I was careful not to make it obvious, but when we came to one of the group photos, Alex spontaneously pointed and said, 'There's Uncle Jack,' and he was right!"

Stories like that did my head in. How could Alex spontaneously remember Uncle Jack when he'd had little or no contact with him, and then point to him in a picture? A year or so later, Mary told me that Alex had come up to her on a number of occasions and said, 'You know I chose you, Mummy? You and Daddy, I chose you'."

The spiritual connectedness of children was becoming apparent to me. Through our discussions, my brother, Richard, had also become increasingly curious about past lives, and the first book he recommended to me was *Old Souls* by Tom Shroder. As an investigative journalist, Shroder was sceptical of past-life stories garnered from hypnosis, but was particularly interested in the work of Ian Stevenson, a psychiatrist attached to the University of Virginia School of Medicine. Stevenson had been researching and documenting children's accounts of their past lives. *Old Souls* portrays one of Dr Stevenson's field trips and some of his remarkable work. Naturally, I then read some of Dr Stevenson's work. To me, he remains something of an enigma. My impression is that he laboured under the weight of being scrupulous in his assessments of every case he documented. He was cautious and qualified everything. This was not a bad thing at all, but his determination to apply irrefutable scientific rigour to his work made reading it onerous. Yet he documented nearly three thousand cases, and on many occasions was able to accurately verify the details of a previous life that a child had talked about. He described children with deformities, and when he could verify their previous lives, the deformities, extraordinarily, often reflected injuries related to their deaths in those previous lives. His research was phenomenal.

My thirst for more knowledge lead me to *Evidence of the Afterlife* by Jeffrey Long, a radiation oncologist whose interest had been triggered by his own patients' stories. Then came *The Truth in the Light*, by a neuropsychiatrist, Peter Fenwick. I quickly bought the texts by Raymond Moody and Elizabeth Kübler-Ross that had been written not long after my father-in-law had his near-death experience. There have been many more since, but in all these books were descriptions of people who in many cases should not have had any persisting brain function and yet were experiencing extraordinary visual and emotional events, often expressed as more real than our world. In some cases, they learned or saw things they could not possibly have discovered while dead or unconscious. The old sceptic in me would have just said they were making it up and dismissed it without further examination, but I could no longer do that. It was too much to ignore.

I had treated patients who had woken during their operations while under general anaesthesia, and their frightened accounts of what happened were nothing like what was being described. I'd seen endless patients who had suffered deliriums, and again, they bore no resemblance to the described near-death experiences. Patients suffering from dissociative states, depersonalisation, and derealisation would sometimes describe a dysphoric disconnection from their bodies, but their accounts were vastly different to those of near-death experiences.

I was starting to set new personal records for book-reading, enjoying thoughts from people like Socrates ("We must follow the argument wherever, like a wind, it may lead us"), Descartes (the mind or subjective world is separate from body and brain), and Antony Flew, a renowned twentieth-century philosopher who had recently abandoned his atheism, who said, "the origin of life cannot be explained if you start with matter alone." Flew also noted that "dogmatic or no-nonsense statements have an air of authority and look at first sight like rational arguments but this does not mean they are either rational or arguments." The dogmatic and no-nonsense bit was an accurate description of the old me. The reading was helping to undo the rigidity of my previous thinking.

Friends' and patients' past lives

10. Now I believe

During the eighteen months following Jenny's regressions, in which I heard my patients' mystical stories, I also performed some regressions on friends who for different reasons were eager subjects.

Anne, for example, had a partner, Scott, who was significantly older and would soon die from a chronic illness. Scott was very spiritual, while Anne wasn't spiritual or religious. She thought a regression might help her see the possibility of life after death, especially in view of Scott's decline.

Anne experienced two past lives with great detail and emotion. The first life was in the 1500s with galleons on the seas and king's soldiers killing all the adults in town and rounding up the children. The soldiers were on horseback with metal plates over their arms and legs. She could feel the metal digging into her side as she, a little girl, was dragged away by the soldiers. The second life was in Scandinavia, probably in the late 1800s or early 1900s. In both lives, she was able to cope with significant loss but recovered and lived happy and contented. At the end of her second life, her recording went as follows.

"I've gone. I'm with my husband [who had died many years before]. I'm young again, about his age. We are just walking through the fields together, remembering all the old times. There are other people coming in, who have passed. They welcome us all together. It's beautiful, like they come and welcome and then go on their way. It's like a welcome. It's peaceful."

It was increasingly evident that people's experiences after death were nearly always peaceful and calming. I was also learning that it was common for patients to remember lives that had direct relevance to the dilemmas or challenges in their current lives, as if their higher self or spirit had chosen to remember those past lives to assist them with those challenges.

Anne wrote to me a few weeks after her regression.

Hi John,

I hope this finds you well.

I really enjoyed the hypnosis session. I've never felt so relaxed as I did that day, after going through the meditation.

I wasn't sure how it was going to go actually or if I was able to be hypnotised. I wasn't expecting to be able to remember all those details and images after the session was completed.

You know how people get hypnotised on stage and act like a chicken or something and then don't remember a thing afterwards? A misconception of mine there.

I did come out of the session questioning myself as to whether I'd made it all up ... but hadn't ever thought of those characters before and I'm not a good actress at all. If I'd only made the lives up I would in no way be able to be so emotionally invested in them. (I'm not that way inclined!) We had it drummed into us as kids to never lie.

With the first life—since then I've been seeing images of costumes and ships etc. that match the 1500s in different books I've been looking at in passing. I haven't been hunting them out specifically. You know—Spanish Armada times and Crusades.

The imagery is still very strongly there—not the emotion anymore though.

I did like my stairs in the meditation. Just like the ones in the Vatican museum. Beautiful. Both characters, from both lives, popped into my head at this stage (had to bring myself back to concentrate on what you were saying twice then). The old Spanish lady (I'm guessing it was Spain now) and then further down a young blond lady.

Strange.

On another note—I've found the books on the Indigo children really interesting too. There are a few out. All quite fascinating.

Anyway I'd best away back to work. Thanks again for all your time and expertise.

Kind Regards,
Anne

As I performed more regressions, I found that it wasn't uncommon for subjects to wonder if they had imagined the whole thing. As in Anne's case, for most others the detail, the emotion, and the spontaneity of the experience made that very unlikely.

Either way, a past-life account often provided a very useful metaphor for, or segue into discussion of, current life problems. I spoke to Anne again some time after Scott's death, and she was pleased to report that the regressions had been very helpful in dealing with that loss.

◆

Until then, I was yet to experience any of my own past lives. I had been meditating regularly, but even with Brian Weiss's regression CDs, nothing had appeared. Then Brian came to Melbourne. Hallelujah!—my chance to experience a past life. My friend Glenn Robbins and I joined the one-day workshop with hundreds of others. The enthusiastic master of ceremonies had spotted Glenn, a well-known actor and comedian in Australia, and microphone in hand, welcomed him to the workshop. Whether being made to feel slightly self-conscious led to neither of us remembering or experiencing a past life, we will never know, but the bonus was that I got to meet Brian.

I did recall a past life one year later. In that life, I was involved with a group of young men trying to create political change in England in the early 1800s. We failed, and in the process one of my close friends was killed. After my death, my soul's message back to me was, "There's a time and a place … whether you are doing things on a smaller scale or bigger scale … you'll know when it's time." It was helpful, as my enthusiasm required tempering. I often needed to use the patience Jenny's masters had told me I possessed in abundance.

◆

Then came Charles, who was a friend in his fifties. A successful businessman, he was struggling with financial pressures, his wife's recurring illness, and concerns about his young adult children. He went into a deep trance in my newly acquired red reclining chair. Charles was lying not quite horizontally, and as soon as he entered a past life, he described blacks and blues and purples and then started to shake all over, especially his legs. This, of course, made me anxious. Was he having some odd abreaction or even a seizure? But Charles kept talking, having identified that he was burning. There was smoke everywhere, and he had multiple stab and spear wounds.

Eager to stop the shaking, I took Charles back to earlier in that life. He then described a Japanese life with lots of men and soldiers, where he was clearly an important figure or leader in his community. On one occasion, attired in red silken flowing robes and with an entourage dressed in black clothes and flat black hats or caps, there was a crowd of people cheering his arrival to a town. Later, in his seventies, he was sitting on a special chair (like a throne) with monks and others sitting down around him. The date 1760 came to him when I asked. At that point, warriors on foot and on horse entered the temple, slaying everybody and burning the temple to the ground. He lay badly wounded and burnt to death, as he had described at the start of the regression.

If Charles wasn't exhausted, I certainly was. When I spoke to him the following week, he said he was "flying" for the rest of that day. I thought to myself that I needed to make sure people were fully grounded before they left the office. Charles also said he was confused by the black cloaks on what he presumed were monks. His understanding was that monks didn't wear black. With some Google research, he had discovered that Japanese monks had worn black, although he couldn't find any mention of the caps. He also commented on how embarrassed he felt talking about his importance in that life.

In his second regression, Charles was born into a Chinese, or perhaps Tibetan, life of privilege. He went through his birth to find himself looking at his mother and realising that she was his wife in this life. As a young man, he was married with great ceremony and had two children (his two children in this life). He then abandoned his family to live as a monk in caves in the mountains. He said he had to follow his calling, but always felt sadness that he had left his family.

While I was speaking to Charles later, he said he suddenly understood why he had always had a voice in his head saying, "You have to get it right this time." He explained that he knew that he had to stay with his family and look after them. I also saw Charles a year later, and he remarked to me that he had suffered from asthma all his life and since the regressions this had resolved. I had read that other regression subjects had recovered from their respiratory illnesses after experiencing a past life where they had died in a fire or from smoke inhalation.

I recognised that it was now time for me to contemplate using hypnosis, and in particular past-life regressions, as a therapeutic tool in my treatment of patients. The first rule in medicine is to do no harm, and I was mindful that these types of regressions were not mainstream psychiatry. Yet I was confident that used selectively and in the right way, regression could have genuine therapeutic benefit.

I had three current patients who had been through near-death experiences, and they were obvious candidates. Judy, who was still very unwell and struggling as much as ever, was one of those three, but came a distant third in my considerations.

Anna was the first, an intelligent and highly qualified woman who had been unable to work for many years. Born to a migrant family, she had endured significant neglect and abuse during her childhood. Her two near-death experiences were a consequence of nearly drowning and then of suffering anaphylactic shock. Throughout her life, Anna had felt devalued and badly treated. Her childhood traumas seemed to have been perpetuated in her adult life despite her determined efforts to educate and empower herself. While living interstate, she had developed a severe depression, with therapy and medication from her previous psychiatrist having minimal impact. Anna had escaped to Melbourne and my treatments so far had also had minimal impact. Anna welcomed my affirmation of her near-death experiences, and after reading *Many Lives, Many Masters*, she was enthusiastic about trying a regression.

In short, Anna had a wonderful response to her six hypnosis sessions. At the start of her second session, she said she was delighted with the first regression.

"I felt like I went extremely deep. The feeling of calm was indescribable—a euphoria or bliss. Since then, I have found it easier to let go of my usual fears. It's like I can see that the fear isn't real."

Anna did go into past lives, "good" and "bad," but also saw a lot of mythic or mystical imagery. On several occasions, she saw a Chinese dragon that she came to realise was her good-luck dragon and companion.

In her final regression, she went back to just before her birth in this life.

"My guides do not like my choice," she said. "They would rather I choose to be the child of my aunt. That life would be hard, but not as hard as this one … but there are lessons I can learn in this life."

Then she illustrated the process involved in entering the fetus, "so I can fit into a baby form."

Following her birth, she said, "All the faces are staring at me. They are all talking excitedly. My guides tell me I have six days to make up my mind about staying in this body."

All the sessions with Anna had an impact. She had discovered that she was an extraordinary spiritual being, but in that final session had revealed to herself that this life was of her choosing. Wonderfully, by then Anna wasn't alarmed by it, and indeed it made sense to her.

Anna documented her experiences and gave me copies. Some examples of what she wrote follow.

After her fourth regression:

> Going into the hypnosis is now a paradox. I really wanted to go into the deep relaxed state but also fear coming back into the real world at the end.

After her fifth regression:

> On the way home I felt as if the energy of the universe was coming toward me. I was being blessed by all the blessing

of the universe. It was all mine, had always been mine but now I started to notice it.

A year ago I would not have believed in past lives/life progression or even known what the field of metaphysics was all about. Now I have read so much and experienced a bit and am really curious about learning more and experiencing more.

I have always been religious, going to church. Believing in human equality, loving others. These hypnosis events have gone way beyond that core belief. This is about SELF love. The very core of the SELF is eternal, divine love and compassion. It is only what we have ourselves that we can show to others.

And:

This between life state of meeting the divine healers, using light energy, music harmony and vibration and just plain love, was so compassionate that I cried. Never, ever in my life had I been treated with such divine worth.

Since those sessions, Anna has come off all her medications. She is happy to take on the challenges that still present themselves, and she remains well.

◆

Jane, in her late fifties, had been a patient of mine for even longer than Judy. Like so many of my patients, she had also had a lousy upbringing. Despite that, or perhaps because of it, she was kind and nurturing, and had worked in childcare between bringing up her own three children. Generalised anxiety was her primary diagnosis, as well as periods of depression. At times of stress, her anxiety escalated to panic attacks. There were also periods when I didn't see Jane because she was relatively stable.

On seeing her for the first time in a while, she reported that her anxiety was out of control again. She also updated me on a near-death experience she had been through during a recent heart attack. She cautiously recounted the details of feeling herself floating out of her body, feeling so peaceful and meeting her deceased father-in-law, who told her that it wasn't her time. I made it obvious that I believed her and accepted that her experience was real. With that, she burst into tears, "None of the doctors believed me. None of them took any notice." Not long ago, I would have responded exactly like those other doctors, I thought to myself. I also knew such an experience was even more likely to be dismissed if the patient had a history of psychiatric illness.

Jane was delighted and our discussion quickly progressed to spiritual matters in general, which seemed even more relevant now that she had suffered a heart attack.

Since her youth, Jane had thought it was likely she had lived more than one life, but like so many people, she had not talked about it much, especially not to her doctors. Needless to say, she was excited to do a regression.

We did three in total. For me, the third was the most profound but the first was the most distressing. In that first regression, I took Jane initially back to the in utero state, before her birth. It made sense that once the soul had joined the fetus, it might feel very connected to the mother or even the father. In this instance, Jane said her mother was singing and feeling relaxed and calm as she rubbed her tummy. Then she said, "But now I can tell she is anxious and fearful. My father is home. I can feel his anger and Mum's fear. She's scared. He's been drinking. He's hit her and hit me."

It certainly wasn't what I expected, though in retrospect I shouldn't have been surprised. It was alarming to consider that Jane's abuse started even before she was born. She told me later that her father never came to see her in hospital after the birth.

Despite those traumas, Jane had remained in her deep trance state. In fact, her normally very worn and worried face had transformed. She looked serene. So I then took her back into a past life where she described herself as a young boy, aged five.

"My skin is dark. I'm in Africa, I think. I'm happy because everyone is happy. They have collected lots of fruit and killed a pig. It's a celebration … they are wearing odd clothes … skins and flowers and horns. My friend wants to leave and do something else, but I don't, because it's so happy and I've never seen this before."

"What are you wearing?"

"Children don't wear clothes. Adults wear something around their waist … it's rough. My mother is hugging me. She's my nanna in this life."

She went on to describe the celebration—the "pairing," as she called it.

I asked her to go forward in time, and the little boy was now thirteen, hunting with his father and others.

"I'm scared. I've got a spear. We are going after a lion. The grass is tall and I'm short. We're running."

Suddenly, Jane, who had been virtually horizontal, sat bolt upright, gasping loudly and clutching her chest. Shit, I thought, she's having another heart attack. Happily, I very quickly found that wasn't the case, as she lay back down and said, "He's picking me up and is carrying me. My father is crying. I can see him carrying me. I'm trying to tell him I'm okay … peace, it's so peaceful. I've been here before. The light is so lovely. It's home. I'm being shown that love and happiness never leaves."

At the end of the session, Jane said she had been hit with a spear.

"It really hurt," she said. "I was in the grass and I could see the lion nearby and I was being told to be quiet. Then we were running and I was following my dad and then the spear hit me. There was too much happening to describe it at the time."

It was not uncommon for people to be so absorbed in their regression that they couldn't verbalise all the events and details. I also made a note to myself — take a Valium before all regressions!

In Jane's next regression, she went back to a happy, contented, and long life in France. Jane was delighted, and I knew the regressions were having a very positive effect. I then didn't see her for seven months, but she rang and asked if she could do one more regression, as she felt there was something important she needed to know or, as I thought later, perhaps something that I needed to know. Of course, I agreed.

As usual, Jane went into a deep trance, and she started with the following account.

"I'm living in a very big home with white columns and a veranda all around. It's America. I'm outside in the veggie garden. It's so hot. So hot."

"What are you wearing?"

"I'm in a white dress, neck to feet. My skin is white, and I'm picking vegetables out of the garden … some sort of potatoes. They are big and odd-shaped and some greens … I'm not sure what they are. I'm taking them in to the cook. She's telling me to sit down and gives me a glass of water because it's too hot. Hm, that's better. I am pregnant. I have to be careful: it's early in the pregnancy. I also have a helper."

"What colour is the cook's skin?"

"She has olive skin … not dark or white."

"And what is the date?"

"It's 1878. I know because it's my birthday today. I'm turning twenty. There's a party tonight. People are coming and my brother John has travelled here for the party. I'm Caroline. My husband, Robert, is ten years older."

"Where do you live?"

"Cape May," she said after a pause. "Robert works in town; does all the paperwork for the businesses. He works hard. He's a good man and loves me."

I then asked Jane to take herself forward to another important time in Caroline's life.

"There's been a fire…" Jane sounded distressed and had concern written on her face as she lay on the recliner. "…a lot of neighbours' properties burnt down. Where's Abby? She's one year old now. Ah, that's good, Nora has got her. John's trying to help all the neighbours … they are staying with us. He is very kind. I'm worried he is doing too much to help everyone."

Further forward in that life: "My son is Robert Junior. John has stayed and is still helping neighbours rebuild their homes. Some are still staying with us. I'm worried about Robert. He's sick and it's getting worse. The doctor says it's consumption. I'm not sure what that is. He's in bed. He's dying. I'm told the children can't see him and I have to be careful."

After her death in that life, Jane's words were, "It's so beautiful. I can see the children around my body. I can feel their love and send them my love."

I then asked her what the lessons in that life had been.

She said, "Love never leaves you. Even when someone dies, they never leave … that love never leaves."

Then, in that spirit state, Jane's guide, Peter, told her that people have to learn for themselves. "Peter is telling me about Darryl [her husband in her current life]," she said, "and that I can't learn someone else's lessons for them."

Out of the trance and grounded, back in the usual consulting chair, Jane was thrilled with the regression.

"My mother was there, too, you know. She kissed me and then left."

Jane was particularly receptive to the advice about Darryl, as she had been concerned that he was too involved in their children's problems. When I asked her if she knew of Cape May, which was what had captivated me, she responded, "No idea. I suppose it's in America somewhere, or was back then."

I was busy for the rest of the day and then raced home to get changed and head to my brother's for our weekly movie night. When Kate and I arrived, I recounted the details of Jane's regression. My sister-in-law, Ali, leapt to her computer and there it was: in 1878, one-third of the town of Cape May, New Jersey, had burnt down.

When I next saw Jane a few weeks later, she still looked happier than I'd ever seen her. I showed her the information I'd gathered on Cape May. She was gladdened, but it felt like I was now preaching to the converted. She knew it was real and that her guides and loved ones were still with her and would always be. After that, I saw Jane about once a year and she remained well. While I was writing this book, I rang her to seek approval to document her experience. She declared that the regressions had been enduringly positive and was delighted that others might read about them. Her only caveat was that I send her a copy of the book.

The Cape May regression and its validation were very powerful for me. That persisting small area of doubt had now gone. I still needed to be discerning, but now I was more willing to look at hypnosis and past-life regressions for some of my other patients. Even, perhaps, for Judy, but it was a big perhaps.

Judy's story

11. You're going all hoogey-ju on me

It was winter and raining outside. Some nine months had passed since I had read *Many Lives, Many Masters*, and I now felt it was time to revisit Judy's near-death experiences. My secretary rang me to say that Judy couldn't make it upstairs because her back was bad. Downstairs, Judy was already talking as she entered the room with a conflagration of grievances, her walking stick, bags, a wet coat, coffee, and a Weston's Wagon Wheel for me.

"The guy at the shop just gives it to me, no cost. He thinks I'm funny," Judy said as she put the inevitable gift down.

It had been about six weeks since I'd seen her, and she was overflowing with complaints and fears. One of her self-inflicted burns had got infected and was healing slowly.

"How did you get here?"

"Train and taxi, and look, somehow I still got wet."

Her hair was wet and had a bluish tinge.

"And just in case you were wondering, that's not Magic Silver White. I'm not that old, but I'm older than I ever thought I'd be. You know, I used to argue with Milly about who would die first. You know … first to the Maggot Motel. I was sure it would be me. I was never going to reach forty-six—that's how old Mum was when she died—and look at me now, over fifty, but there'll be no Magic Silver White.

"Milly is your cousin, is that right?"

"Yeah, I don't see her as much now. She's one of the few members of that paedophile family of mine that I like. John, my back's fucked. My leg and my foot are numb. The neurosurgeon says it's nerve compression but doesn't want to operate. And the pain is still bad. I'm going to end up in a wheelchair."

"James's got you regularly on the morphine patches, hasn't he?"

"Yeah, but it's still bad."

"So would it be better if he stopped them? There's no point being on them if they don't help."

Sometimes I couldn't help myself and had to push back on her negativity. I also thought the morphine patches were as much about numbing her psychological pain as her physical pain.

"Now you're being smart," she said. "And I couldn't sleep."

"Worse than usual?" I enquired.

"I ran out of tablets, John, and I've had no sleep for days. He's such a tight-arse."

"Who's that?" I asked, knowing it was probably her doctor.

"James, he just doesn't get it. Stick-by-the-rules James. He treats me like a drug addict, and fuck, now I can't talk froffly."

For a moment, Judy's mouth and lips looked like they were doing gymnastics. Her mouth was obviously dry and her top lip kept sticking to her teeth. She reached over and drank from the takeaway coffee next to her.

"I've got drought mouth. My lips stick to my dentures."

"Judy, you know we are just trying to limit how much medication you take. If you take too much, it just works against you, and you're already on a truckload. And they are probably contributing to your dry mouth!"

"But I ran out."

"Because you'd been taking too many."

"I get desperate."

"And does taking extra help?"

"No, but now I've got none."

"Honestly, I think James is a good doctor and wants the best for you."

"Sure, but if he tells me one more time to find an extra five percent… You can do it, just find an extra five percent," Judy said in a sing-song voice. "Oh and 'smell the roses'! Fair dinkum, one more time with the roses and I'll tell him where he can jam them. And John, Stacey's pregnant. I can't believe it. And now she says she wants to have nine. Bullshit. It's hard enough with three. Don't know how she'll cope with four."

Today was clearly not the day to re-examine Judy's spiritual experiences.

A few sessions later, I finally found the moment to raise the topic of Judy's near-death experiences and the possibility of at least trying hypnosis for her pain and perhaps even for her smoking, though I had to admit that might be a tall order. It was a cool day with soft blue skies, the odd almost translucent wafting cloud, and a warming sun. Judy was in a more positive mood and her hair was in a ponytail, albeit hanging on one side with short hair on the other.

"Judy, I've been thinking recently about those occasions when you nearly died: when you were out of your body and saw the gold light and got told it wasn't your time and then told you had to look after the kids."

"Yeah, and I figured—well, that's stupid, because I've only got Stacey and can't have any more. And now I've got her and the three grandkids. And fuck, John, I had to look after all three of them last week. Stacey had a job for the week. They need the money, but now I've got none and I'm stuffed. I like to cook for them, but…."

As usual, Judy had veered off-topic, but I was pleased she had fairly regular contact with the grandchildren now that Dylan and Paige were no longer in her care. Judy was always worse when she was living alone.

"So, you do remember those experiences, when you were floating at the top of the room?"

"How could I forget? I was up in the corner of the room. I can still remember how peaceful it was. I don't know why I didn't turn around to look at the light where the voice was coming from."

"So, I've been doing a lot of reading lately and listening more carefully to my patients, and I think what you experienced was real, not just some drug effect or brain discharge."

"Yes, it was, it was bloody real, it was grouse. And John, nothing like what you feel on drugs. It was so real. I remember it all."

"So I figure that the light and the voice was some sort of spiritual being or guide or something like that communicating with you."

"I've never told you, but I felt like I knew who it was, like it was really familiar. That's weird, isn't it?"

"No, not at all. In fact, it makes sense. I think that after we die, we often meet up with people we've known in this life and other lives."

"Knowing my luck, there won't be anything."

"On the contrary, given what you experienced with the gold light, it strikes me that they are telling you that is exactly what will happen when you leave this body, or this life."

I presumed she didn't hear the comment about other lives or chose to ignore it. I was eager to talk more about the topic, but had to tread carefully. I certainly wasn't about to suggest that she had chosen this life, although I presumed now that she had. With Judy, I felt it was very important to engender some hopefulness. So if in doubt, repeat yourself, I thought.

"You know, I think that's exactly why you had those experiences, to let you know that there is life after death. You saw the doctors using the paddles, trying to shock your heart back into action. It makes sense to me now that life goes on even after you die. So the only thing that goes to the box condo is your body. I reckon your soul or your spirit joins the others. I'm pleased that you can remember how good it felt."

I now genuinely believed that Judy's near-death experiences were a vital part of her trajectory, but at the same time, given how close she often was to suicide, I paradoxically didn't want death to sound too attractive.

"But now that Stacey's pregnant, I suspect you are going to be spending more time with the grandkids. There's more for you to do in this life."

"John, you're going all hoogey-ju on me. You've never talked like this. Maureen will love it."

"Yep, I have to admit it's a big shift from what I used to think. Sometimes I'm still shocked by what I believe now, but I can't change it. So, part of what I've been looking at is hypnosis, and I'd like to try hypnosis with you and see if we can help the pain and maybe even help you stop smoking."

"The smoking! Good luck with that ... but why not? It costs me a fortune," she said, with her animated face somewhere between a frown and a smile.

Not only was her smoking siphoning away a huge part of her weekly pension, but both Judy's parents had died of vascular disease and she was now a prime candidate for a heart attack or stroke.

"You're not going to make me do something weird, are you? Quacking like a duck and all that."

"Hypnosis is really interesting. Even if you are good at it and can go into a deep state, there is always part of you that is conscious. So you won't do or say anything that you don't agree with. If you are good at it, we can maybe use it for other things as well."

"How about weight?" she asked as she glanced down at her seated body, which looked a little squeezed into the multicoloured skirt she was wearing.

"Yes we can do that, or teach you how to do self-hypnosis or meditation for the pain, or just to get you more Zen—more relaxed."

"I trust you. If you think it might work, then sure."

I then performed an eye-roll test on Judy that suggested she was very likely to go into a deep state.

"Judy, I think this could be really helpful."

"Okay. So when do we start?"

"Let's see how you go at our next session."

Judy proved to have an outstanding ability to go into a deep trance. I kept the first session to a healing hypnosis with a focus on relieving the pain. As she came out of the trance, she announced, "John, I've got no pain. No, really, it's gone. I could do cartwheels!"

"Please don't do that," I said nervously. "We can do it again next time if you'd like to."

"Hell, yes. It's the duck's nuts. I feel great."

As she headed down the stairs, I could hear her telling the secretary she was pain-free.

The pain relief didn't last forever, but Judy reported that it persisted for four or five hours after her appointment. Her next few sessions included more hypnosis to relieve her pain, and I gave her a few guided meditations that I had recorded on CDs. They had proved helpful with other patients, and Judy loved them. A few months on, Judy was confronted with having another pap smear.

"It's filth, John, I can't do it. I hate it."

"Would it be better if James got one of the female doctors to do it?"

"No, it makes no difference, and I trust James, even though he can be a dick sometimes. But John, it's filth. Why can't they wait a year?"

"It's been more than two years, Judy. It's well overdue. I want you to use the meditation. When you have the smear, take yourself into the garden like you do with the hypnosis and in the meditations. You are so calm in that state, and can go there quite quickly now. Tell James what you are doing so he can give you a bit more time before he does the smear."

Judy came to her next appointment triumphant.

"It worked. Fuck, what a spin. I was in the garden and I could hear the waterfall [Judy loved waterfalls], and then it was done. But it's still filth."

When the results came through, Judy was happy that nothing more needed to be done.

"James said things weren't exactly normal but were okay. But John, there's something I've never told you."

I held my breath. Those words always made me nervous.

"Ever since I was a teenager, I have scrubbed down there with a toothbrush."

In that moment, Judy's melancholy eyes looked even more sorrowful. I was shocked and yet not shocked, and, as always in these situations, immediately sad and a bit speechless.

"John, it's filth. I had to do something to clean it."

"So just on the outside, or inside as well … in the vagina, I mean?"

"Both, and especially inside. I have to make sure it's clean."

"How often?" I asked, trying not to give away too much of my distress, while hoping she would say "once a year." It was hard to imagine anyone feeling so contaminated that they could attack themselves in that way.

"Every day, of course, in the shower. It's filth, and I have to clean it, but there's always still a discharge."

"I'm sorry, I'm a bit shocked. It's awful that you felt that you had to do that. And to be honest, it must be damaging the skin and tissues down there."

Knowing that Judy's education had been very limited, I added, "By the way, it's quite normal for women to have some vaginal discharge. You should ask James, and he'll…"

"John, I've used toilet paper down there since I was a kid. I knew it had to be infected. I put the toilet paper in my knickers to get the discharge. It was filth; I knew I was disgusting."

"Judy, it may well be that the discharge was quite normal. I'll write to James and ask him to discuss it with you further. I know you saw yourself as contaminated because of the abuse. And I know they physically hurt you."

Judy interjected with a mixture of sadness and rage. "John, sometimes they made me bleed."

The old trauma was always there, and I was still struggling to help her find some peace.

"Judy, you were little. We have to find a way to be kind to that little girl. It wasn't your fault, and you're stronger now and not contaminated. Scrubbing yourself in the end will only make you feel worse."

We then discussed hypnosis for her smoking, and I was already wondering if hypnosis might be useful in tackling the scrubbing behaviour.

Judy had a great response to the hypnosis for smoking. "I tried to have one but I started gagging," she told me later. "Even the smell makes me feel sick. You're a genius."

"Actually, it's you that is the genius. It's your subconscious that's decided not to smoke. And it's the same with the pain. You just didn't realise you had that power."

I wasn't about to give Judy a lecture on how Franz Mesmer had thought it was his special powers that mesmerised people and put them into a trance. We know now that the hypnotherapist is just the facilitator. In the end, it's the patient that chooses to let go and get in touch with their subconscious or higher self. For some people, it's easier than it is for others. I remembered Jenny's masters saying to me, "She's recognised she can do something that everyone can do—they just don't know it."

To this day, Judy has essentially remained off the cigarettes. Every now and then, she would have a small lapse that was easily fixed with a top-up hypnosis. She also used the hypnosis to stop the toothbrush scrubbing. As an adolescent Judy's uncle had commented on how much he liked her pubic hair. Ever since then she had shaved it. The hypnosis had finally allowed her to stop this habit as well.

Despite her morphine patches, when things became very stressful, Judy would still occasionally use heroin. The hypnosis again proved successful in dealing with this. She admitted she tried it a few more times but just felt "stupid" and "got no benefit."

Judy's life never seemed easy. A breast lump freaked her out.

"John, it's the dancer. I couldn't cope if I was lopsided."

It proved to be benign, but she later fell apart when two dear friends died. The first was Milly, her cousin, who had argued with her about who would die first.

"She used to visit me in hospital. She was very kind."

The second was Evan, a young man who Judy befriended. He also suffered from drug dependence.

"No, John, really, he was like a son. I loved him. Lung cancer. Go figure."

Despite the gains she had made from the hypnosis and her increasing spiritual perspective, her only solution was to burn herself again. As always, I was fearful she would take it further.

Stacey had her fourth child, this time a boy, and Judy was surprisingly cautious. "I'm scared to get close to the younger ones—if I get too close, I won't cope if something happens to them. Boys get abused too. That's what happened to Evan."

Her fears aside, Judy still often found herself looking after the children, sometimes spending up to a week looking after all four of them.

I finally decided that I had nothing to lose and that I would try a regression on Judy. There was no question she had been through more than enough trauma to explain her psychiatric disorders, but even with all the treatments, she remained unwell, continued to physically harm herself, and remained at risk of killing herself. She was receptive to a spiritual point of view but was still swamped by her past and her self-loathing. I hoped the regressions might allow her to see her current life from a higher perspective, know that it was just one of many lives, and really know that she was loved. The regressions might even lead to a discovery of who she really was and what her spiritual goals were in this life.

I had now performed more regressions on patients, and suggested the regression to Judy. Her response was like that of many others.

"If I've had them [previous lives] I must have been pretty bad. Otherwise, why would I have had to go through all of this shit?"

"I just don't think it's that simple. From what I've read, and from all the people I've done regressions on, it varies enormously. Sometimes the lives are traumatic, sometimes very simple, sometimes complicated, and sometimes loving. I just haven't had anyone famous yet. I honestly don't think it's as simple as being some sort of punishment. In fact, I think we've probably all had lots of lives, and we've been good and bad and everything in between. When I see someone doing something that really annoys me, I now say to myself, 'I probably did that in a past life.' Sometimes I have to admit I've probably done it in this life! I think with each life it's a chance for us to experience something new, to learn, and maybe become more enlightened. And when we do regressions, I think our subconscious or our soul shows us past lives that will be helpful in dealing with this life. And Judy, sometimes people don't see a past life, and in that case we will just do a healing hypnosis like we've done in the past. I think it's worth a try."

I was surprised Judy had let me talk for so long. I was also careful not to try and define things too much. I liked certainty, but when I read material that was too definitive or strident, it started to feel like religion. I knew I still had a lot more to learn.

"I'd give you a few books to read, but I know you don't like reading much."

"Nah, it's not my thing. It's a spin, but I want to see what happens. I know I really like it in the red chair, and you're the Big-Picture Projectionist."

Hopefully, I thought to myself, the regression will provide an even bigger picture than the one she gets from me.

"And John, those CDs you gave me are scratched. Can I get new ones?"

12. What the fuck?

> My religiosity consists of a humble admiration of the infinitely superior spirit that reveals itself in the little we can comprehend about the knowable world. That deeply emotional conviction of the presence of a superior reasoning power, which is revealed in the incomprehensible universe, forms my idea of God.
>
> *Albert Einstein*

◆

In the first regression, Judy initially went back to her childhood in this life. She was a little girl in her cot.

"Chris Bell is there!" She looked and sounded fearful, and I was suggesting she float above that scene when she became aware of her father in the room. "He is protecting me but doesn't realise it. He loves me. I'm safe now."

I asked Judy to float above that scene, and explained that while still in that deep state she could go even further back in time—back into a past life. She did exactly that, and I was jubilant.

"I'm wearing a brown dress. I'm cooking ... sort of like a street stall, big pots hanging from a tripod over a fire. I'm cooking and selling food to other people. I have three children ... two girls and a boy ... they are playing next to me."

"What else can you see?" I asked.

"It's a small town, a saloon … and a barber. There are other people cooking outside as well. It's like I'm in a western. And there's Indians."

"How old are you?"

"I'm forty. My husband died … it was alcohol and a fight."

Judy looked sad and about to cry.

"But my sister's here. I'm tired. I have to look after them."

"Who do you have to look after?"

"My children."

I asked Judy to go forward in that life. I sensed that she was taking it all in but was not easily able to describe it.

"I'm older. The children are adult and all close. We live with my sister and her kids and her husband. He works with cattle. We are all in the one house. One daughter has a beau. We are all close. I'm still cooking and the children work with me."

I asked how she was dressed.

"In a dress with buttons in the middle up to my neck."

With her next move forward in time, she went to the end of her life.

"I'm old, in bed. They're all around the bed. I'm sick, something like whooping cough. I don't want to say goodbye, but I know they love me."

"I'm floating above my body now."

It was odd seeing Judy lying calmly, without her usual agitation.

"How does it feel?"

"Peaceful. I can see them around the bed, crying and sad. The light, I'm going to the light, I'm letting go of that person, that personality. The light is beautiful and bright, so bright, but I'm not scared. I think the light is someone…"

I then asked Judy if there were any messages or lessons from that life, and looking so peaceful, she said, "It's about family and love and to keep going."

After the hypnosis and a period of orientation, Judy exclaimed, "John, I was really there. And there were real Indians. That doesn't seem right, does it? And I was cooking in huge pots hanging over fires. Weird. And John, I was skinny, not fat. Shit, if you'd asked me who I would have been back then, I would have said a big black mama for sure."

"And your daughter had a beau?"

"Yeah, get fucked. As if I'd ever use that word."

Judy delighted in the regression, and I was so pleased to see it broaden her view of the world and herself. A few months later, she requested another, and I was happy to oblige. In a deep state, she quickly went to a past life.

"I've just had a baby, given birth. It's outside under a tree. It's a beautiful day. There are people around, but not close. A lady is helping me. She is black and the baby is wrapped up. It's white and I'm white. It's a boy, and everyone is happy. I have four girls, and this is the first boy."

In stark contrast to her normal speech, Judy often spoke very softly in her hypnotic state, and I sometimes had to ask her to repeat what she had said. Having done that, I then asked, "What is the date?"

"It's 1802. I'm not sure. That's just what I see."

"And your name?"

"It's Eileen. I'm twenty-one."

"What can you see around you?"

"I don't know. We are outside. There are no hospitals. There are a couple of timber or wooden buildings I can see. A lady is bringing over my children, the four girls. She has been looking after them. They are in long dresses down to their feet, with bows. Everyone is happy because it's a boy. My husband is very good to me. He will be happy. Now I'm holding the baby."

"Do you know where this is?"

"Not sure what country. We are in the country. The boy will be called Mark. My husband is Mark. I have long hair in a bun, but now it's messy. I can hear a tapping sound in the distance. You know, like a telegraph or something. I'm not sure."

I wondered if this represented the era she was about to live in: some time after the mid-1800s.

Going forward, Judy continued to describe that life.

"Two of my daughters are teachers. It's a very little school. There are only six or eight benches in the room. There are no books. They write on little blackboards. I'm proud of my daughters. All the children are around me. They call me Grandma, and are tugging on my dress."

As Judy spoke of the tugging, she started pulling on her own dress as she lay on the red reclining chair in my office. Actions like that seemed to indicate the extent to which she was embedded in that memory.

"It's the grandchildren, and I look after them when my daughters teach. I'm very happy. They call me Grandma."

As she spoke about the grandchildren, a broad smile appeared on her face. I didn't need to ask any questions, as she continued to illustrate the scenes and feelings of that life.

"Mark still lives at home. All the girls are married. We have a farm and are well off. We grow produce—lots and lots of fields of corn."

Judy began making a rotating action with her hand.

"I make flour, and bread from the flour to feed everybody. There are big pots in the kitchen. We have cows, and horses, and carts. The stables look like a postcard. It's America. My husband is very good."

Judy went forward in time again, and this time she suddenly became very sad, and a small tear rolled down her face.

"My husband is dying," she whispered.

"What illness does he have?"

"Tuberculosis. We are all around the bed, the children and grandchildren and friends. Everyone is dressed in black. He is eighty. He is older than me. Everyone is sad. He has loved me and I love him. My second-eldest daughter is Stacey in this life."

After that, Judy went forward to the end of Eileen's life.

"I'm dying, in bed, all the family with me. Mark is holding my arm. Everyone is sad, sad to say goodbye."

When Eileen died, she quickly found herself lying in healing crystal waters. I asked what the lessons were in that life, and she responded, "To be there for family and to love them."

Out of the hypnotic state and grounded back in the room, Judy was a mixture of joy and bewilderment.

"Wow, I've been with Stacey before. And, John, my husband was Mark and I called my son Mark. No fucking way. That's the middle name of my most abusive brother—the name makes my skin crawl."

"Not something you would have made up, then," I suggested.

"No way," Judy said, looking incredulous and yet gratified.

Judy's positive response to the regressions was very reassuring for me. In fact, over the next two years, while life was hard, she managed better than she ever had. Even my wife, Kate, while still enjoying the Judy anecdotes, took great pleasure in hearing of her progress.

The regressions were obviously important in giving Judy the knowledge that this was not her only life and that she had lived other, happy lives. If I thought about why those lives had been chosen, it made sense that both lives strongly reinforced the importance of her own family—Stacey and the grandchildren. It was as if her soul, or guides, knew this was what would sustain her in this life.

During those two years, Judy often found herself looking after the older two children, and sometimes all four. Her life didn't suddenly become easy, but her load seemed a little lighter, and there was less anger and less self-reproach. She enjoyed talking about the regressions and connecting them with her near-death experiences.

A further regression didn't appear necessary, but we continued to regularly use hypnosis for pain, and Judy remained off cigarettes and heroin, and no longer scrubbed. The next step was to stop her narcotic patches. James agreed and so, again using the hypnosis and some of Maureen's "hoogey-ju meds," Judy came off all narcotic medications.

Soon after, Judy, still with her usual flourish, came into her session wearing a beret.

"I like the hat," I remarked.

"I love hats. You know that. I've got heaps of them, all on the hat stand in my bedroom, next to the sign on the wall that says, 'Good morning, let the stress begin.' And John, the kids have got nits. I always have to treat them when they stay with me. And there's no space, my unit's only got two bedrooms. When I've got all of them, some have to sleep in my room. So Ian's going to help me apply for a three-bedroom place."

Ian was one of the gems in Judy's life. He was a solicitor who often helped Judy with government or legal matters. By now, Dylan had taken up permanent residence with Judy, and in due course she received some government financial support. Just as Stacey's childhood had been full of separation and uncertainty, Dylan's had also been messy and often riddled with change. Stacey loved Dylan, but had been struggling with the load. Judy, who also clearly loved him, was now able to give him a comparatively stable base.

"Oh hey, I nearly forgot…" With that, Judy pulled a plastic cylindrical container out of her bag and gave it to me. Inside was the neatly rolled skin from JW's latest shedding.

"He wraps around me twice now. Show Mrs Webber. She'll love it."

"I'm not sure about that. What do the kids think?"

"They love him."

We went ahead with a healing hypnosis, but this time I followed one of Brian Weiss's scripts, where she met her spiritual guide, who was able to show her events from the past that might help her to deal with her current troubles. I didn't ask or expect Judy to say anything, but suddenly she started talking.

"It's Mum. She's holding me. I'm a baby, all wrapped up. She loves me and is showing me off—showing me to her parents and sisters. Her Italian family."

I let Judy experience that joy as long as I could. Later, sitting back in the consultation chair, she was beaming and crying.

"I never thought she loved me, but John, it was real. She loved me."

Even a week later, Judy was still embracing that love.

"I just feel so much better. I know she loved me. She was showing me off. It was at George Street, my grandparent's place. I know I was really loved. She was so proud. But John, I'm tired. I had all the kids last weekend."

Judy remained uncommonly well, and would intermittently make statements like, "I know I've changed and I'm stronger," or, "I can't believe the change. It feels like it's worth being here. I love enjoying simple things." And a few times, "John, I think I'm becoming boring. I don't even swear as much. I don't want to be boring."

My response to that was easy.

"Seriously, I don't think there's much risk of that."

At times, verbalising how much better she felt led to tears.

"I don't hate myself as much, and the kids know I love them, even Stacey."

Even when her responsibilities and stressors were overwhelming, her expanded and stronger sense of self now allowed her to tolerate the emotions that would previously have led to self-destructive behaviour. She knew that her near-death experiences and regressions were real and that she had been loved, in this and previous lives.

I remained delighted with Judy's progress, but knew she still had lots of vulnerabilities. And of course, it made sense that after decades of feeling and behaving a certain way, sometimes she might slip back.

"Sometimes, the old thoughts come back, and I still get so angry. But I want to live so I can be with the kids."

Perhaps predictably, Judy then met a man called Jeff. He was five years older, had been divorced years before, and had two adult children.

"John, I was buying tickets to the wrestling. Dylan loves the wrestling."

I had to admit, my heart sank a little when she mentioned the wrestling. But then I reminded myself that I had gone to Festival Hall when I was a kid to see Billy White Wolf use his sleeper hold to defeat the Beast. It was great fun, and I had watched the Beast have all his hair cut off as the agreed penalty for his loss. Not such a big deal these days, with a buzz-cut now fashionable.

Judy was still talking. "He's a nice bloke and wants to take it slowly," she said.

Taking it slowly was not one of Judy's strongest traits, but the relationship progressed and a few months later she declared, "It's the first time I've had sex with someone and not felt forced. John, I didn't go back to being that little girl."

Judy then became tearful. "But I'm scared of getting too close. I'm scared of being hurt."

"All you can do is take it one day at a time. Don't jump too far ahead. If it's good now, let yourself enjoy it, but the most important thing is that you are true to yourself."

"I suppose I'm just not used to it."

"And Judy, remember the only person that really needs to be okay with you … is you!"

"You know, we had to take the bus to get here today. The train was cancelled because of a suicide on the train tracks."

Hearing news like that always made me feel sad, and at the same time perversely hoping it wasn't one of my patients. Judy could see I was distracted, and as I regained my attention, she said, "You know, I think I understand now what effect that would have on others."

◆

Neither Judy nor I were satisfied with just the two regressions. Judy wanted to know what other lives might surface. I was equally curious, and wondered what might reveal itself in the spiritual dimension. I had now performed even more regressions, and I was very drawn to the wonderment that people felt in the spiritual state after going through the death of a previous life. I also had fewer reservations, as Judy had clearly benefitted from the previous regressions.

So with Judy back in the red chair and in a relaxed hypnotic state, I asked her to let her subconscious mind choose the time, whether from this life, a previous life, or between lives when she was in the spiritual state. Unexpectedly she again went back to a time in this life.

"We have to choose. Mum and Dad are fighting. Dad is hitting Mum. We have to choose who we go with. Chris says both—he's trying to choose both."

I asked how old she was.

"I'm four. I'm wearing jodhpurs and a jumper and Jelly Beans on my feet. The jodhpurs and jumper are green. All the boys are there, trying to choose. I can't choose. She hates me but I can't choose."

Judy was distressed and crying. I didn't ask for any more details, and instead suggested she float above that scene. I offered that she could take herself further back to before she was born—when she was in her mother's womb.

She did exactly that, and without speaking, Judy immediately looked calm and relaxed until a deep frown transformed her face.

"He's hitting me. It's not Mum; Dad's screaming at Mum. He's hitting her, and I'm in her tummy."

I asked Judy why she had chosen this life.

"To not be like that. To love … real love. I don't want to be that. I'll learn."

I then explained that she could go through her birth to when she was born, without any pain or discomfort.

"Mum, my mum, she's crying. Dad's not there. She's hugging me. I love you, Mum. She's crying because she's happy."

Judy was also crying.

"She loves me. She's saying, 'My little girl'."

Leaving that scene behind, Judy then recalled a previous lifetime.

"France … it's war. I'm French. We are against…"

I asked what she was wearing.

"A grey button-up coat—it's cold—full-length, shoes, gloves, walking along a river and helping people. I'm hiding the French people … I've got a house … they're scared."

"Are you male or female?"

"I'm male … it's my home. The people … I think they're French. I have a skinny house. You can get under the house. That's where they hide. I can hear the fighting nearby, shots and bombs."

I asked how old he was, and his name.

"I'm nineteen… I'm Anoir, and I'm married. Three boys. I'm proud. Twins aged four and a little one."

The name wasn't familiar to me. It could have been Anoir or Anouar or Anwar.

"And your wife," I enquired.

"She's lovely. Georgia. The kids are playing upstairs. We are hiding only three people. The soldiers are knocking on the door. The children are quiet. They would kill us all…"

At that point, I sat up straight, as if trying to relieve some of the tension in the room, not to mention my spine. After a significant pause, Judy spoke again.

"The men we were hiding have left and the Germans are looking downstairs but they've gone. We are all safe, they are safe but the Germans hit you. Their presence scares me … hit me with the gun in the face but it's alright … they got away. They're all safe."

"What are the names of your children?"

"Ardene, Jacques and Bubba … the baby I call Bubba."

I then asked Judy to take herself forward to another important time in the life of that man.

"They've shot me. I'm twenty-two. I'm rising above it. Oh no, I'm not leaving … I have to. The kids are crying … they love me, crying over me and Georgia holding me in her arms and saying, 'don't die.' Shot in the stomach, below the heart. Shot for hiding people … other men."

Judy was sounding distressed.

"They're shooting them … they're all dead. I couldn't protect them."

Judy then went back to the garden with a waterfall. Relieved to see her face look more peaceful, I took a sip of water from the glass next to me, and then asked if there were lessons she had learned in that life.

"Always help, to look after … you have to be there for the ones you love, no matter what. In the end, they were there for me."

After a brief pause she then continued. "I'm floating to the light. A beautiful light, peaceful."

She looked serene, and then, talking to herself, she whispered, "What's next … the next life? I'm four again. With poor parents, but they are happy … in England, in the streets with other children."

I looked for more detail. "Are you a boy or a girl?"

"A little girl, Jenny," Judy laughed, "dressed in a pinafore with puffy sleeves. I don't look as smart as the other kids, but I like it. They are more refined. I think I look good."

I was enjoying Judy's engagement in the details and emotions of that childhood.

"I'm hitting a ring with a stick." Again she was laughing, "I've never seen that … and the ring rolls and the kids hit it back."

"Do you have a brother or sister?" I asked.

"A little brother, John, he's a pain sometimes. Mum's calling us … cabbage soup. It's awful but we eat it. We are all at the table. It's a wood-fire stove. She's cooking over it, a big pot of cabbage."

I continued to request more details.

"Mum's in a long dress, long sleeves, buttons, and an apron on top. Little shoes with heels, but not like those ladies wear who are posh. Dad is a skinny, tall man, dark hair, skinny but strong. I like it here."

Jenny went on to have two children and died aged sixty with her husband applying cold compresses to her coughing and choking body, with her children at her side.

Her second life as Jenny was clearly a loving and happy one. Her French life, though, had ended very traumatically, and I was concerned about its impact on her. Out of her hypnotic state, Judy opened her eyes, paused a moment, and then, as only Judy could, looked at me and said, "What the fuck? You didn't tell me I could be male!"

She had assumed that in all her past lives, she would have been female.

"And my mum, I saw her holding me. She loved me. She loved me. I knew Dad could be cruel to her, black bastard and all that, but even when she was pregnant? But John, he never touched me."

At her next session, I showed Judy a Googled image of children playing with a hoop and stick. She was again incredulous.

"That's unbelievable. John, you know I barely went to school, and you don't learn that stuff from watching *Neighbours*."

As usual, Judy's revelations delighted me.

13. Forgiveness

> Forgiveness is for yourself because it frees you. It lets you
> out of that prison you put yourself in.
>
> *Louise L. Hay*

♦

My practice remained very busy, and I continued to explore the spiritual side of things with patients when it seemed appropriate and they were receptive.

A number of the past-life regressions I had conducted with patients had been very therapeutic. Some came out of the regressions wondering if they had made it up, but without any recollection of having done so. Even for those patients, the past life or lives often provided an excellent metaphor for conflicts they were experiencing in their current lives, and therapeutically, that often proved very helpful. I hadn't detected any detrimental effect from these discussions or the regressions.

Some patients were eager to experience a past life but were frustrated when nothing came. One such patient was Laura, who had a busy married life with four children. Laura had obvious psychic abilities.

She recounted a story to me regarding a recent trip to the snow. "It was just a day trip with another couple and their kids," she said. "They were always disorganised, and when we got back to our cars at the end of the day, they couldn't find their car keys. My angels or guides or whatever you call them told me where they were. So I told my friends they were at reception of such and such a lodge. They didn't believe me because we hadn't been there. Anyway, James headed off while we kept looking. The keys were at that lodge—someone had handed them in! My friends now ring me whenever they lose something, and sometimes I can help."

Recently, Laura had come to her appointment appearing a little distracted. Having sat down, she looked at me quizzically and said, "So, are you a twin?"

"No," I replied, somewhat taken aback.

"That's weird," she declared. "When I was here a month ago, and again today, I kept getting 'twins' coming to me."

I just smiled and then explained, "Well, as it happens, just before your last appointment, my son and his wife had twins. They are my first grandchildren and they are twins, in fact, identical twins."

"Ah, good, that explains it," Laura said rather nonchalantly.

Laura was eager to know about her past lives, and with the hypnosis went into a deep trance, but when it came to the point of going back in time she later told me that her guides said, "Nope, nope, nope … not for you." She explained that it felt like they were telling her she had the psychic abilities and that was enough for now.

♦

Kate and I would sometimes take time out from the noise and intensity of the city and spend a weekend at a little shack we rented down on Victoria's surf coast. While there, I awoke one Saturday morning with a message persistently repeating in my head. "You have to love yourself. Really, really, really love yourself." The message reverberated with a lot of what I'd been reading and was coming through loud and clear. Later that morning, while sitting with Kate on the veranda, I closed my eyes and meditated on that thought: really, really, really love myself. About five minutes later, Kate said, "Don't move quickly, but just open your eyes." As I did that, I saw a large, beautiful butterfly sitting on my chest. It stayed for a few minutes and then flew off. I closed my eyes again and returned to the meditation. A few minutes later, Kate told me to open my eyes again, and there was a different butterfly resting on my thigh. The universe, it would seem, thought the message was a good one.

♦

Judy's chaotic life was continuing unabated, and she could still get distressed and angry, but was clearly stronger. Psychiatrically, she had not required a single admission to hospital since the spiritual element had first been included in her treatment over four years earlier. It was now nearly a year since Judy had recalled her life as Anoir, and we agreed it was time for another regression. An extra-long appointment time was booked because a short debrief of Judy's recent ordeals was always needed, and then the regression itself could often continue for over an hour.

When Judy came to the appointment, she was in good spirits. Her hair was streaked with red. Her walking stick was now a mandatory part of her ensemble, but she was moving so freely it was hardly required. She was on time, as she nearly always was now, and it was clear she had remembered we had a regression planned for the day.

"Jeff's not sure about the reincarnation stuff. James … John … fuck, I saw James yesterday. I had to see him about Dylan."

"So Jeff's not sure?"

"Look, he's pretty good, he's just not come across it before. I tell him that you should be doing this with everyone. And you should, John, it's magic. Seriously, who would have thought … Judy Bell with past lives in America, France, and England. It's a spin, but it's more than that. I can't explain."

"I know it's a lot to get your head around. Not just that you've had past lives, but there are lives in the future as well."

"No, that's bullshit, I need a rest."

We covered a bit more about Dylan and Jeff, and then started the regression. I was now using a rapid induction technique that saved time, and as usual, Judy quickly went into a deep state. As she started to remember a past life, I asked her what she had on her feet.

"Black shoes. Everyone else knows but I don't understand the game. There's a board with holes and five cards."

I posed the usual questions about her sex and age.

"I'm seventeen, male, in a castle … trees everywhere outside, there's a war happening. Soldiers outside the castle, with metal clothes, with helmets, oval and rounded and pointy at the front."

With both hands, Judy was tracing the shape of the helmet, rising up to a point at the front.

"And your name?" I asked.

"I'm Jeremiah. The master is teaching me. He runs the school. He's teaching me on my own. The others have gone."

"How are you dressed?"

"I'm wearing blue and white, royal blue, and crisp beautiful lace at the top of my neck. The master is more frilly around the neck … a robe, it's green and frilly around the neck and chest part."

With her forefinger, Judy was now drawing vertical wavy lines from her jaw down to her chest and then back up, as if to describe the ruff.

"The master is green like the trees. The master is you. It's a big room and he's at the end of the table and he's jovial, he's good."

I asked Judy what the date was.

"It's 1602. I'm seventeen."

"Do you live in the castle?"

"It's a school, I don't know, there are lots of people doing other things, and soldiers. There are big beautiful pictures on the wall. They look like old pictures of young people, portraits and big chairs."

I asked Judy to go back to when Jeremiah was much younger in that life, and her recollections then painted captivating images and emotions.

"I'm wearing funny little pants," she said, smiling broadly, "like balloons but little ones … and white, shiny white. I'm in a dress for a christening or something—lace and shiny and white and long. I'm in my mother's arms. My father, he's not around much, he's in the army. He's at the christening but he's leaving. They are all going, the soldiers. There's war. My mother is always around but others care for me … the black lady there and others."

Jeremiah's sister's name was Antoinette, and his mother was called Contessa.

"She has a skinny waist. Her dress flows out, big, out to the ground, on top it's buttons and embroidery, a lemon colour and just beautiful, just beautiful."

I was struck by the fact that Judy never swore during the regressions, and her speech revealed a clarity and focus that was in stark contrast to her normal, distracted dialogue.

She went on to describe Jeremiah's life.

"My father died in the war. It's over. It was us, Spain, against … I don't know … it looks like England."

When I asked who won the war, she didn't respond.

"He was very strong and he was good to his men, but a lot of them died. Now there's a woman with me. I'm nineteen, she's seventeen … a suitor. We are getting married. She's off with the women. She comes from good blood. Everybody likes her. I live in the castle. I've been there for a while."

"Is the master still there?" I enquired, wondering if "I" was still in the picture.

"He's always there, shining. When he talks, he glows. I'm working out the cards. I'll get there. There's a lot of people."

At the end of that life, Judy described the transition simply.

"It's hard to breathe. I'm old, old. I'm in a white bed, a wooden bed, but everything is white. Antoinette is there. I'm fifty-two, still in Spain. I'm dying."

She was silent for a while. Then, "I'm rising, the people are crying, and I'm looking down on them. I'm sad, but it's better than being sick. I'm moving up. It's beautiful. It's amazing, like air, but you just float around lighter than air."

Occasionally, I would ask simple questions like, "What happens next?" or "What are you experiencing?"

"It's Chris Bell, John."

I think that was the first time she had used my name during a regression, but she was anxious and distressed, so I responded.

"Stay with that scene. You are quite safe. You are safe now. Is that his spirit?"

"Yes," was all she said.

My mind was going at a thousand miles an hour, but I asked what seemed the logical question.

"What would you like to say to him?"

"Why? Why? I know none of us had it easy, but why?"

He was obviously communicating with her as she explained.

"It was resentment. He resented that Dad bashed him and the boys, and it was his way of getting back at Dad. He's very sad. He seems blank, but not like I've ever seen him."

"Is there anything else that you want to say to him?"

My mind was still racing. And then, quite extraordinarily and emphatically, Judy said, "I forgive you. I do forgive you."

It felt like an eternity passed, but I was grateful, because I was lost in the profound nature of what had happened. Eventually, I added, "Does he hear your forgiveness?"

"He tries to touch me, but just touch me on the shoulder. That's enough. It's alright."

I then added, "Allow yourself to enjoy that spirit state."

"They're showing Dad's funeral, his body in the coffin. I don't know … if he had treated me differently. I don't know … but it's all better. And Mum is there and she's crying, she was quite sad. I don't blame her. She's sobbing."

Still trying to digest it all, I asked if anyone else was there.

"Madrina, my godmother. They've got faces but they haven't got faces, but you can tell."

As she spoke, I remembered that Jenny had expressed a similar sentiment in that spirit state.

"We are see-through," Judy continued, "like rays of colour, like blue, green, yellow, beautiful colours, bright and happy. We are all made of these colours.'

"And you?" I needed to know if Judy could see herself.

"Bluey and turquoise. You can see their faces but you can't. It's in your heart… They're saying I'm fixed but there's other things later on."

"Because of the forgiveness?" I almost blurted.

"Yes, yes it is. Yes, I forgive. It's beautiful."

Somewhat insatiably, I asked if there were any other messages.

"I think that's it," she replied.

How was this possible? Forgiveness of Chris had never been on the agenda, but there it was. Judy was fully alert now, but our session time and my lunch break had vanished. I was exhausted, but Judy was radiant, though looking perplexed and needing to elaborate.

"It was so real and so beautiful. I understood what he said and I just wanted to forgive him. I needed to. John, it was real. I can't explain. Something has shifted. I feel great. And the colours … everyone had different colours and I could tell who they were. It was like someone had gone around with a paintbrush, splashing colours over the whole world. John, I really feel like I've forgiven him."

We had to finish, but my mind was racing with thoughts of my presence in her past life, of Spain, of neck frills, card games, curved helmets, suitors of good blood, of colours, and most of all of forgiveness.

During the week that followed, my thoughts and my excitement charged ahead unabated. I contemplated Judy's soul communicating with Chris's soul. Chris was still alive, but I was comfortable with the concept that part of our soul is with us in this life and probably the larger part is in the spirit state or engaged in our other lives. So why couldn't Judy's soul be communicating with Chris's soul at a higher level?

Judy obviously had very little background knowledge of spiritual issues, and this made her accounts even more compelling. Her descriptions of souls and their colours and knowing who they were, like Jenny's, were magical. At our core, we are simply light and energy and consciousness.

The other details of the regression seemed less important, but the card game intrigued me, as I had been taught cribbage by my father as a boy, and my research revealed that the card game was played in the seventeenth century, and its predecessor, "noddy," before that. I also printed pictures for Judy of sixteenth- and seventeenth-century Spanish soldiers and their helmets, as well as the ruff of a Spanish gentleman of that era. Noting how large and uncomfortable the neck frills looked, I wondered if that was why I had never liked wearing polo-necked jumpers.

When I saw Judy a week later, she remained slightly overwhelmed and yet joyous. This time, before she could sit down I asked, "So, have you heard of cribbage?"

"No, what's that?"

It was evident Judy didn't have a clue what I was talking about, so I explained the game.

"And John, you were there, the master, teaching me the game. Everyone else had learned it, but I was slow. You were very patient."

Then I showed her the prints of the Spanish soldier and the gentleman. Judy was nearly speechless, but not quite.

"Fuck me. That's exactly how it looked. John, John, I've told you I didn't do geography or history. I don't know any of that stuff."

"I understand," I said, and I really did believe her. "But tell me, how are you feeling about Chris?"

"You know, I used to imagine all the ways I might punish him—like skinning him—I used to dream about it. I was going to pay for his funeral so I could stomp on his grave. I know it's weird but I just have, I've forgiven him. I just can't get angry about it anymore. It's not like I want to see him, but it's okay. That's his journey. Shit, I'm going to be boring."

From that time on, Judy's fear of Chris and her other abusers dissolved and her forgiveness remained. It felt like I was witnessing a miracle. It was enormously gratifying, but not something that I could keep to myself, and I was relieved to be able to share the joy with Kate. I also knew I needed to stay grounded, even though I was blissfully unaware of how our journeys would continue to unfold.

14. Back to the future

> For us believing physicists, the distinction between past,
> present, and future is only a stubbornly persistent illusion.
>
> *Albert Einstein*

◆

Melbourne's weather was warming up but, typical of spring, one day it was
warm and then the next day cold or raining. It had only been three weeks
since the forgiveness regression, and Judy and I were both still basking
in its glow. Judy arrived sporting a pretty green-and-blue-patterned scarf
wrapped around her head and tied in a bow above her forehead. She looked
younger as she started to speak.

"John, it's still a trip out. It's a huge load off. I feel lighter. I can't believe
I've done it. It's not just Chris, it's Mum and Dad too."

"What does Jeff think?"

"Yeah, he's pretty cool with it now. Dylan likes him. John, I had all of
them, all four of them, for three days. Tiana gave Dylan such a hard time.
She's tricky; she doesn't listen to me. And Stacey gives me heaps. I worry
about her, but I ring her every day. Can we do the red chair today? I need
it. I think I'm addicted. I just want to stay there. And my back's fucked,
I need it for the pain."

After a bit more discussion of recent events and what strategies she
might adopt, Judy made her way to the red chair for a healing hypnosis. In
her usual deep state, and experiencing herself bathing in the healing waters

of an ancient sea, she started to smile broadly. Her eyes remained closed but then she turned her head fairly suddenly as if paying attention to something over her left shoulder. We had used the same script on numerous occasions but this was quite new. She looked like she was engaged in something fun, so I didn't ask her to speak and let her enjoy whatever was going on.

At the end of the session, I asked her what had happened.

"I was talking to my guide. We were having fun arguing about the future. I told him I wanted to go home and he said, 'No, you have another ten years or at least ten years.' He was funny."

"So your guide is a he?"

"No, not really, but sort of. He's a beautiful gold colour, over my left shoulder."

I was curious that Judy had used the term "home." It was not an expression I had used. It was intriguing for me because I had just finished reading *The Journey Home*, a parable I had interpreted as representing the pilgrimage of discovering who we really are. I was also learning that nothing is coincidence.

I wasn't content to leave it there, so at Judy's next session we used the healing hypnosis again, and this time when she turned her head, which I had eagerly hoped she would, I asked her to say what she was experiencing. She then started to illustrate a future scene.

"Everyone is there. It's Tiana's sixteenth birthday. They're all there. Dylan, Paige, Tiana, and Callum and Stacey. They are all good and they're all big. I'm now not the big one! Tiana and I are close. I've bought her a stereo. She loves it."

I wondered if Jeff was there, but didn't ask. Instead, I enquired about where the party was being held.

"It's a lovely big white building. It's not a house. Callum's annoyed that I'm giving Tiana so much attention."

I knew that Tiana was around six years old, so Judy was being shown an event about ten years into the future. I asked if there were any other messages for her.

"I have to give Tiana a break and don't be too hard on her."

This was all very new and unfamiliar territory. None of my patients had gone into or been shown the future before. Then again, it was Judy, so why be shocked? Trying to be logical, I decided that I could consider it one of Judy's possible futures, but there was a lovely certainty attached to her portrayal of the party. She had now been told by her guide that she had at least another ten years to live, and then was shown an event ten years into the future. Beyond my amazement, there was also the question of why this was being revealed to her.

Back in the normal consultation chair, Judy was briefly silent, so I let her think and then asked, "What are your thoughts?"

"They were all there and I was standing," she said. "Fuck, if I last that long, I figured I would be in a wheelchair for sure. Tiana and I were really close. John, she drives me crazy. I can't see it happening."

"Well, I suppose your guide wants you to know that you'll be around in ten years and is showing you evidence of that."

"And John, I wasn't the big one."

While still a bit on the heavy side, Judy's weight had been pretty stable over the last few years. It varied, but nothing like in the past, and I presumed this was due to her improved emotional state.

"And the gold, I want to find that so I can show you. I've been looking but I can't find it. He told me I won't find it here."

"You mean here on Earth?"

"Yeah, he's funny. He's always over the left shoulder. It's beautiful, really beautiful."

Sadly, the appointment time was over and I was going to have to wait. Judy's appointments were now weekly or fortnightly, and I had learned to book her sessions before my lunch break so if we went overtime, which was common, it didn't affect the rest of my day too much. My practice was still busy, and while I was inclined to ask about the spiritual or metaphysical experiences of most of my patients, the majority were still being treated in the traditional way. For the minority, exploring the spiritual side had proved a very helpful addition to their treatment. I liked the idea of doing more of the spiritual work, but I concluded that that would happen when the time was right. Recently, one of my psychiatrist colleagues had referred two of his patients for past-life regressions, and the outcome had been very affirming. He had enjoyed *Many Lives, Many Masters*, but reading Eben Alexander's book *Proof of Heaven* had provided extra impetus. Another psychiatrist friend had joined me at one of Brian Weiss's weekend seminars and had decided to learn to use hypnosis and explore her own past lives.

I was contemplating writing a book myself, but tended to dismiss the idea because I'd never been a writer, I didn't have time, and of course there was always the fear of judgement. Despite that, ever since Margot had given me *Many Lives, Many Masters* more than five years earlier, I had religiously recorded events and thoughts in a journal. I had also recorded and transcribed nearly all of the regressions I had completed. Kate, who loved reading, had already made her feelings clear. "If you want to write a book, I think it should be about Judy. That way, the story is engaging, people can see the benefits, and you can still include other important details. It needs to be about you as well. But only do it if you want to."

Kate's own spiritual journey had led her to focusing on the positives. She loved the teachings of Esther Hicks and Abraham in *The Law of Attraction*, as well as those of Louise L. Hay. I had been amazed watching her negotiate two mastectomies and chemotherapy for a metaplastic cancer of her breast some eighteen months before. The tribulations and challenges of that odyssey hadn't dinted her beliefs; in fact, if anything, they were stronger. So when it came to the book, she would simply say, "If it brings you some joy, then go with it."

When Judy returned two weeks later, I was eager to go back to the future, but that was not to be. She looked slightly agitated and preoccupied. She made brief mention of the outfit she had bought for six dollars at the op shop, but then got straight to the point.

"Stacey's been looking at my mum's background and she says she wasn't Italian. John, she was Aboriginal, one of the Stolen Generation. She's been checking it out for a while. She found out from Chris Bell's kids. I don't like her hanging out with them, so I wasn't interested. But it's true. It makes sense—her black curly hair, her flat nose and dark skin."

"You're kidding! Struth, that's a lot to take on-board."

"No, it's real. And John, I've been thinking about it. The lies—everyone lied. Everyone. Why?"

"If it's true, I suppose everyone was ashamed." I couldn't believe we had gone so quickly into a new crisis, or at least a possible crisis. I wasn't immediately sure how this would affect her, but she had obviously already had some time to contemplate it. So I continued. "People were even more prejudiced back then. We forget how bad it was. I presume they were embarrassed and thought people would look down on them. Look how long it took for you to talk about your own abuse."

"Fuck. Poor Mum. Fuck. But I like being a wog, and now I'm a Koori."

"Judy, you will always be a wog. That was your upbringing."

Being a wog was one of the few positives in her childhood, and now she was at risk of losing that.

"So now you'll be a wog and Koori."

"Fuck, the lies. And Dad, that's why he called her a 'black bastard.' He lied."

"It's a lot to take in."

I was repeating myself, but I realised I wasn't just talking about Judy but my own capacity to digest what was happening. I could see how her mum would have blended with an Italian family, and with that background, no one, including myself, would have doubted Judy's heritage.

"So I suppose half or a quarter of your genes are Koori. I know it's weird, but to be honest, it's the same for all of us. We are all a mixture. And you're still a wog."

"Yeah, but it's a spin. I don't know what's true. Poor Mum."

Time would tell, but there wasn't much reason to doubt what Judy was saying. I also admired that Stacey had pursued the issue and was continuing to forge her own path.

"Can we do the red chair?"

"Not today. We won't have time, and I think we should talk a bit more about you being Koori as well as being a wog."

Despite her protestations, I could see that Judy was already adjusting. That ability to adapt was at least in part a consequence of her improving self-esteem and resilience, as well as her spirituality. Paradoxically, the discovery also helped to explain some of her childhood memories. It also wasn't unfamiliar for Judy to feel connected to a minority. The hardest part for her was accepting the deceit. She felt as if she had been part of perpetuating that lie. During our discussions, she mentioned her dad a few times and in response I suggested, "Maybe he thought he was protecting you?"

"John, he wasn't a great guy, I know that now."

Outside, I could hear the neighbours' dog barking as if in agreement.

"Don't forget we are all capable of lying. We do it to protect ourselves, but sometimes we think we are protecting others."

"Yeah, but it sucks. And I chose all this. Fuck me."

I had to admit I liked it when Judy brought things back to a spiritual perspective. By the end of the session, she summed up her thoughts: "It's mental but it makes sense."

It was soon after confirmed that Judy's mother, Marjorie Bell, had indeed been one of the stolen generation of Aboriginal children. Finding out about her heritage, combined with going to Stacey's wedding, caused Judy to crash over the next month. She wanted to give Stacey away at the wedding but, as usual, it was complicated.

"Two of Chris Bell's kids will be there and maybe he'll turn up. I've forgiven him but that doesn't mean I want to have anything to do with him."

"I take it Jonesy isn't giving her away?"

"John, she's only seen him twice since we separated when she was a kid."

"Are you serious? He's only seen her twice?"

"Yep, that's Jonesy. He told her he had to find himself. I don't think there's anything there to find. What a … yeah, I know, it's his journey. John, I can't even get properly angry anymore. But he is a dickhead."

I was incredulous. It made me appreciate even more the challenges that Stacey had faced growing up.

"I hope it works out for her with Ryan."

"I don't trust him. I know, I know, it's her choice. And John, I was going to get some heroin. It's so easy to get. Don't worry, I didn't."

The switch in mood from positive to negative was obviously bringing back some of Judy's old insecurities, so I felt some explanation would be helpful.

"I think what happens is when you've been feeling happier and then something really stressful happens—like the Aboriginal stuff and now the wedding—none of it's really bad, but it feels worse because things have been so good. It's a big contrast, but you're not back to where you started."

Judy survived the wedding, and, in fact, meeting two of Chris Bell's children was liberating. At her next appointment after reviewing the wedding, she declared, "I don't think I can do the hypnosis, because when I do, I don't want to leave. It's too nice."

"Are you practising at home?"

"Yeah, it's nice, but not as good."

It made sense that she could go deeper in an environment where she could be guided and felt safe. Looking over at the red recliner, she then said, "No, I have to do it. I need it."

We weren't to be disappointed. Again, immersed in that relaxed and highly focused state, she started to communicate with her guide, and the initial message was for me.

"He's telling you you've got a big journey. You have to tell everyone about this and you know you have to. But he said you know that."

This was the first time the communication had been directed at me, so I took the opportunity. "Are there any other messages for me?" I asked hopefully.

"'It's as one' … he says that you'll know what that means."

I did know what that meant. Nearly everything I had read, and information I'd gleaned from all the regressions, suggested that we are all connected and in the end we are all one. If we hurt someone else, we are hurting ourselves.

Judy was having fun again. She was attempting to pass on what was happening, or at least, I was attempting to find out, but sometimes it got lost in translation. On a couple of occasions, she smiled and said, "He's funny."

Again, her language was often different to when she was "awake." In truth, I thought Judy was more awake in the hypnotic state. At one point, she remarked: "He said men aren't bad, people aren't bad, you aren't bad," and then, "Now he's taking a stick and drawing in the sand. It's been a rollercoaster, he says, but now it will always be above the line."

Later, and still smiling, she said, "He's showing me Tiana's sixteenth birthday again. My hair is brightly coloured. I'm a colourful Nanny."

Their conversation continued unabated, though quite suddenly her smile faded.

"He's telling me the drugs aren't the answer. That's why I fell in front of the policeman. Drugs aren't the answer. They're band-aids and band-aids fall off."

By the end of the session, I was in desperate need of some clarification. Once Judy was alert, I poured her a glass of water. Drinking helped to ground her, though, like most of my ADHD patients, she would have preferred coffee. Then, I enquired, "So can you draw me what he drew in the sand?"

"I'm going to call him Goldie because of the gold colour. It's so beautiful."

"That sounds good. Here's a pad. Can you draw for me what he drew?"

Judy then proceeded to draw.

"John, I don't understand why I was above the line at the beginning. It's always been bad."

"No, it hasn't. You remember when your mum hugged you after you were born, and how much she loved you, and when she was showing you to her family?"

Judy was smiling again.

"And John, Goldie [obviously the name was going to stick] showed me Dylan travelling overseas, Paige finishing school, and Tiana starting secondary school, and Callum—he's naughty, controlling everything."

"So I think he is telling you that you are going to be okay and that there's things to look forward to—that you're going to be around for at least ten more years. You'll be at Tiana's sixteenth birthday and you'll stay above the line. I like it … but what's with the policeman?"

"John, remember I nearly used again? Well, I was in the city and thinking about it, and then I fell. When I got up, there were two policemen right there."

"I don't think that was a coincidence."

"I know, I know. Band-aids—and band-aids fall off. Fuck me, I can't hide anything. And you know, you've got the same gold around you. When I came out of the hypnosis, when I opened my eyes … it was the same gold all around you. It's like you're him, or connected somehow. It's happened before, but I didn't say anything. And sometimes when I'm doing the healing, you both say the same thing at the same time. It's quadraphonics!"

The gold colour, I presumed, was similar to the amber colour Jenny had seen around me. The idea that I was connected to Judy's guide was rather overpowering. In fact, initially it felt somewhat grandiose, but I realised that that was my ego talking. Who's to say that all of us, all souls or spirits, hadn't taken on the role of guide at different times? If I was to believe that the larger part of my soul, or what some call the over-soul, was in the spirit state, then why not? Why not be a spirit guide as well? In my heart, I believed we are all connected, which is exactly what Judy's guide, Goldie, had said to me at the start of the session: 'It's as one'. I was certainly aware that I was on a big journey but, as part of that, Goldie had said I had to tell everyone. Initially, I had been impatient to do exactly that but, as Jenny's guides had said, I needed to learn more, go with the flow, and enjoy myself, as everything would come in its own time. I would contemplate all this and more over the coming weeks, but right then I had to end the session, as we had gone well over time.

"Judy, we have to finish up."

"I know. And John, you had that same glow in the Spanish life, when you were my teacher."

"Well, that makes sense. I believe you, but we really have to finish."

"I think I'll call you little Goldie."

"I accept that I'm connected to Goldie, but I'm good with John for the moment. Now, we have to finish."

Judy was in the often prolonged process of packing up her belongings— the walking stick, her glasses, the shawl, and one of the packets of biscuits she had bought at the train station. The other packet was sitting on my desk.

"Judy, don't forget your phone."

I picked up her phone and gave it to her. It had gone off loudly during the hypnosis, but Judy had remained oblivious. As she walked out of the room, standing a little too close to me, she said, "Band-aids—no more band-aids. I have to tell April, she's lovely, John, but she's still using."

"Judy!" I said firmly, feeling a little frustrated and time-pressured.

"I know, I know. You know that I really appreciate what you do?"

"I do, and thank you. I'll see you again soon."

Holidays and Christmas intervened over the coming months. Judy remained happily involved with Jeff, and often surprised by his support of her. She was engaged with friends and doing her best for Dylan. She was always worried about Stacey and the other three grandchildren, but more accepting that what limited help she could provide was valuable.

During hypnosis sessions, Judy continued to have humorous conversations with Goldie. Sometimes, the messages were simple: "Just take each day as it comes." Sometimes, he was specific: "Keep an eye out for April and support her." Sometimes, it was more abstract: "You are never alone. You never have been. Even at the worst times, you are never alone." On occasion, Goldie would explain things to her: "You had to experience the anger and hate to learn forgiveness."

At the end of one hypnosis session, I had said it was time to leave that state but she could return there in the future. Her face immediately reflected her disappointment, and she said, "He's thrown a handful of colour at my head. He's laughing and telling me not to be so dramatic. He says I can be very dramatic."

Dr John Webber

15. I am my mother

You are not a single "you."
No, you are the sky and the deep sea.
Your mighty "Thou," which is nine hundred-fold,
is the ocean, the drowning place
of a hundred "thous" within you.

Rumi

◆

Both Judy and I were curious to see if there were any other past lives on offer, so we agreed to do another regression. From my point of view, it was also about the between-life insights. As always, she easily went into her deep state.

"I'm dark-skinned. A girl is chopping wood with an axe, no handle, just the stone, which is very sharp. Some have vines around them to hold onto it better. One woman has a special one, with a wooden handle and vines and seashells attached to it. It's special. You hit the wood, fast and jabbing.

"The little girl is annoying. She might get burnt by the fire. The big girl pushes her away. They are mixing herbs with hands for cooking … cooking boar caught by the men. Chris Bell is one of the men. He killed the boar. The little girl has another father, a white man, and doesn't fit in."

At this stage, I wasn't sure who Judy was in this life, and I'm not sure she knew it either, but then it became evident.

"There are horses and a cart. The cart has high sides, but not at the back and front. Some of the other children are taken as well. I'm told to get in. Why isn't she coming with me? Why? No, no, she has to work. The man is telling me, 'Just get in!' I go to the corner. I'm so scared, I just want to scream. I'm so scared."

Judy had tears streaming from her closed eyes.

"My sister is yelling … She'll get me … She's yelling she'll see me in the end. They don't take her. She's too old. We are younger."

"What else do you see?" I asked.

"The men are cooking. A boy has come of age. They are cooking pork. The menfolk got it."

"What else?" I thought the details were important.

"A little river. Joannie used to take me, my sister … the river just nearby, we get the water from there but we played, throwing things at each other and into the water. She said she didn't mean to be nasty. She used to get cross with me."

Judy went forward. "I'm being told to get in the truck. Awful men."

"How are they dressed?" I asked, still trying to orient myself.

"Big pants with rope. They are all white people. The bad one, he's got Aboriginal in him. They hit the kid. I'm holding on because I don't want to fall."

I asked Judy to take herself forward in that life.

"I've been taken to a family by a woman in a big coat down to the ground and a hair net. I smell food cooking. The man is nice, he's old. She's nasty. There's other kids … two others." Judy was obviously taking herself forward as she spoke of that life.

"She treats me bad, but not them. And hits me. The older one is like her mother. And a boy, not one of them, he's nice to me and tells me not to worry."

I asked how old she was. Anyone looking from the outside would have seen my slightly hunched posture as I listened closely to Judy's responses as she lay in the red chair.

"I'm seven."

"And how are you dressed?"

"Not like them, with pretty clothes and shiny shoes and a ribbon. Not me. I've got this thing on, but it's clothes she gave to me."

"And the little boy?"

"He's from down the lane, past the policeman's house."

"What's your name?"

"Marjorie. She gave it to me. She's not nice. The man gives me food and takes me up the shop. On the corner, there's a big building on a big road. We sit there and watch the carriages with horses."

"What does he buy you?"

"Twisted candy." Judy laughed. "And he tells me to hide it. He's yelling we've got to get home. The porch … I have to clean it with a little brush … before I go to sleep."

At this stage, I was contemplating that Judy was experiencing her mother's life. Her mother was named Marjorie. It was likely that Judy had also drawn that conclusion, but I chose not to ask. She went forward again, this time to when she was seventeen.

"I work in a tin factory. We make tins for food for the war. I've met a sweet, sweet man. I meet him at the market. He says he'll take me away."

I had to ask his name.

"Bernard."

That indeed was Judy's father's name.

Judy spontaneously took herself forward.

"He's changed. Lots of children, boy, boy, boy, boy, and I'm pregnant again. He's punching and hitting me. It's the same as everyone else. I want my sister. She said she'd see me but she's not. He's awful."

Judy then again took herself forward to her own birth. I was struggling to grasp what was happening, or, to use Judy's words, I was spinning. My earthly assumptions about how things worked were being fiercely challenged.

"I've got a girl. I'm in hospital and I'm having a rest. We've called her Judy. Bernard wants that."

"How do you feel?" I enquired.

"Finally got a girl. I'm pleased. She's number eight. I'm going to Mum's place for a rest."

Judy jumped forward to that time.

"We're walking in the door. Nanna's got the bags. I can see my room. She kisses me on the head. It's the first time, the only time. The little girl, so tightly wrapped. Nanna loves her because she's a girl."

For a moment, it was as if Judy was caught between the feelings of her mother and her own feelings as a baby. I was barely saying anything. I didn't need to, and I was starting to consider the possibility that Judy and her mother shared, or were part of, the same soul.

"Pop … he's having the medicine. It's a decanter, he says it's the medicine. It's whiskey. He loves the little girl. He loves me. Mum loves me. The sisters are buying pink for the baby."

Once again, Judy took herself forward without prompting.

"I'm getting up off the bed. I have some soup. I haven't eaten for a long time. Been sick."

"What's wrong?" I questioned.

"Don't know. Hardened liver or something. Everything, really. Oh, the pain, it's not like the other…"

"Where?" My own voice was croaky while Judy's was soft.

"The heart."

After a pause, Judy finally spoke again.

"I'm passing over. It's beautiful… Yes…" Judy sounded delighted. "It's my sister. She's been here a while, waiting. Beautiful. I'm looking back down at the house. I haven't passed fully over. I've gone but not fully gone. Ah, the kids, they are all out the front. It's beautiful, better than ever. They are crying, and Judy, I'm sorry for her. He loved her too much. It's beautiful, bright lights. I've noticed you. You're there, very bright. You're telling me not to be scared. I'm following that light. I'm thinking of the kids way back there, the boys and Judy. I'm with my guide … with you. You are my guide. I was loved, I am loved, I'm not alone, I'm never alone. I'm in a big room; it's got glass bits made into pictures and it's all… Everyone has come today. Everyone is in the room. All colours, they are colours."

"What colours do you see?" I responded, still feeling dumbfounded by the unfolding drama and details.

"You're gold and yellow. I'm trying to look at my own colour. That's hard. I'm looking at everyone else. Yellow ones, green ones, and lots of purple."

"Do you know the beings?"

"Yes."

"How do you know?"

"They've been down there with me." Judy was smiling broadly. "The man who used to talk to Dad and I outside the pub at the end of the lane." Judy was clearly amused. "He's up here with me ... my little ray of sunshine."

I had to keep reminding myself that this was simultaneously Marjorie and Judy's soul in the spirit state. I then asked if there were lessons to be learned in that lifetime.

"It's a relief. I had to trust, but I couldn't trust that family like the family back home. But the little one, she was good to me. So I had love— maybe it's love—from Martha, the little one, who was younger than me. It's so good up here. There's Mr Neale, the neighbour up the road. He's brown, not a good colour. He was a paedophile."

I couldn't help myself, "How do you feel toward him?"

"There's no bad here. Understanding, that's what I've learned: to understand and to care."

"What happens next?"

"The wall is alive but it's not alive. A hole opens up. It's not a door as such, but it's a hole, and we go through it." She laughed. "He went through it and came back in to show me I can do it. I can't, I can't do that. Oh, it's beautiful, peaceful, colours all around. I'm staying."

Wondering what other lives Judy and her mother might have lived, I asked, "Are you aware of your other lives?"

"Yes." She chuckled. "Hiding them from the soldiers, a big knock at the door. They check everyone but they didn't find them. All of them are coming ... one I was ... no one hurting me. I've got two children. Everyone runs after me, helping me, doing things. I'm very royal. Ah, yes, and he is so suave, my husband. We are royalty, and I get treated so well, even by him!"

I then asked Judy one of the questions that often proved fruitful.

"That spirit is you. Is there anything that spirit would say to you in this life as Judy?"

"It's telling me to love and trust, really trust, and that it's going to be okay. And happiness ... I'm happy, probably for the first time. No, I can see a bit of happiness in every one of them, in every one of my lives. Sometimes a little bit, sometimes a lot. To trust and to love, and you have to trust to love." Judy was laughing. "And now he's saying to love myself. One day!"

I presumed that she was talking with her guide, Goldie. We were well and truly out of time, and foolishly I asked,

"Is there anything else?"

Judy was again shown details of Tiana's sixteenth birthday, and I liked it when she mentioned Stacey. "She's still telling me off," Judy said. "Oh, but this time she's telling me the right place to sit."

How was all this possible? It immediately felt unbelievable that Judy's soul could also have lived her mother's life. I was comfortable with the concept that we could have overlapping lives. I also accepted the idea that time is an illusion, as Einstein had stated, and that we may well be living all our lives concurrently. But to be yourself and your mother at the same time? That, surely, was a bridge too far. Perhaps Judy was being shown her mother's life—tapping into the collective unconscious. From my perspective, there was no question that she had been in a very deep state and experienced her mother's life. It was as if her guide, Goldie, had already pre-empted my confusion when he told me, "It is all as one." If, at the end of the day, we are all one, then of course Judy's soul could have been living her life as well as her mother's.

Judy emerged from the hypnosis with a flood of questions.

"What the hell? John, so that means I was my mother. That's too weird. And John, she never saw any of her Aboriginal family again. But I saw her sister after I died, my sister, fuck, whatever. And you were there, or Goldie, the same gold. Beautiful. I love it when I am there."

As always, I was curious about the details.

"Did you know where your mum worked?"

"I know she worked at a place called G. or J. Gadsden's."

"And making tins or cans?"

"Wouldn't have a clue."

But those details weren't important to Judy. What she had experienced had been clearly profound.

"John, something's shifted. Something's different."

Over the next few sessions, Judy and I discussed the implications of the regression. While astonished, she was surprisingly comfortable with the conclusion that her soul had experienced the life of her mother. She felt a connection with her mother, or herself, that had never been there before. Perhaps most importantly and wonderfully, this also allowed her to be forgiving of all her mother's failings during her childhood. In the end, I think I had more difficulty adjusting to the concept than Judy. I pondered the idea of being my own mother, father, sister, or brother. If I accepted that we were all spiritually connected, then why couldn't that connectedness include our soul living the life of someone like our mother? I was slowly getting my head around it.

Fortunately, my struggles to comprehend these concepts were being helped by other patients and their regressions. The critical information often came when they were in the spirit state. For example, Angela, who had been very curious but initially sceptical about past lives, had recounted an eighteenth-century life and described events after her death beautifully. Her recording went as follows.

"I'm just in space. It's peaceful. There's a light on my left. I do feel good. I'm moving toward the light slowly, like swimming. It's generally dark, it's like when you float, feels free. There's nothing, but it's good. The light is there. It's good. I know I should go toward the light. I'll go later. I'm moving toward it slowly. There are other lights, too, like dust spots, the same light but further away … little balls of light. I'm one of them. We are all moving toward the light, but really slowly."

I asked if she was connected to them. "Separate, but as we move into the light, we all become part of it," she responded. "Mm, there's no rush, it's good. Still floating, like an astronaut, no rush, just floating. I'm in the light now. We are all in there, we are all the same, all part of it. I feel bigger. We become the bigger light. And there are shapes, like 'being shapes.' We are all changing now. There are so many. We are all together. It feels so good. Some move away. I'm not, not yet."

I asked if there was any communication with the other beings.

"We are all one. There is communication."

Another patient, Cassandra, had a regression that I'd recorded, which also remained etched in my memory. Cassandra suffered from recurrent depressive episodes, and also had longstanding ruminations about global conspiracies. Her past life as a man in a Britain devastated by Roman invaders drew some powerful parallels with her conspiracy fears. After his death, in the spirit state she said, "I'm being told, love everything and everybody. You are everything and everybody. There's another thing I keep hearing: love is around for a reason. It caresses you. We are our own fetus. We are the womb and the fetus, and there is no distinction. We sustain ourselves, and that's why we have to be aware of the importance of each other. It's like I can feel an umbilical cord that attaches us back to ourselves. I am my mother; I am my child."

Having got lost in the mother/daughter dilemma, it took me a while to recognise that the most important psychological aspect of Judy's Aboriginal life was the losses she had suffered. It helped explain her uncommonly powerful response to loss in this life.

In the meantime, Judy's complicated life progressed with her being as happy and as well-functioning as she had ever been, at least for the moment.

Dr John Webber

16. The wisdom of Goldie

> The first problem for all of us, men and women, is not to learn but to unlearn.
>
> *Gloria Steinem*

♦

As she came up the stairs, Judy was already talking. She had brought Dylan with her, and he always looked embarrassed, yet amused, when Judy was in full flight.

"John, I need a coffee. No, really I do. Dylan's got his iPad, so we are good to go."

They were slightly early and my previous patient had cancelled, so we *were* good to go. Wanting to keep consultations professional, I was strict about neither making coffee for patients, nor drinking mine while with them, but I did make the occasional exception. Coffee in hand, Judy had already chosen the subject of our consultation.

"I want to do another regression. One more. I think I got shown a royal one when I was being shown all the others. Anyway, I need the red chair."

For some time now, I had been recording all of Judy's hypnosis sessions, not just the regressions. I'm not sure it was the royal life she had spoken of, but Judy did go back to a most wonderful, loving, and generous life. This "royal life" was an English life in the nineteenth century, where she had been adopted into a wealthy family. She went on to explain, "I was given to this family. They treat me like one of their own … given to them by my parents. They didn't have money … it was done then."

Her adopted family were very wealthy, and yet she would still see her birth parents.

"I see them when we go into town to do the shopping. My father was a bit of a drunk. I'm much better off with this family."

She had a sister and a brother with the new family, and was clearly loved and treated as an equal. As a young woman, she described getting dressed. "You have to do up the corset, can't do them up yourself."

"Who helps?" I asked.

"The lady. She helps us all. One lady for us girls, and mother has one."

I enjoyed listening to the vivid details of her schooling, fine clothes, travels, and happy marriage. Her father and husband were in "the banking business … high up in the bank … very successful."

Of her brother, she said, "He still seems very little, with his peaked cap. He worked in the bank but didn't like it, and became a farmer. He grew corn … corn, of all things. Father came to accept it. Mother can be pretty persuasive."

At her daughter's tenth birthday, her parents invited all the "townsfolk."

"Mum and Dad like everyone. There's Mrs Harrod, who owns the general store. Her store is so cluttered, old jars of food and pickles." I was struck by the poignant contrast this life revealed when compared to her Aboriginal one.

Judy went on to describe events following her death.

"Ah, it's beautiful. I'm leaving the top of the room with my guide. Up, up, and whoosh." Then, after a pause, "There's life on other planets. Not like humans." She was laughing. "They are funny little things. I'm being shown that to open my mind."

I asked what she had learned from that previous life.

"Yes, to trust and not to judge, never to judge, because everyone has a story."

Then, in conversation with her guide, she continued.

"I'm asking if things get sorted out with Stacey, and he says life's a journey and you learn a lot on the way. She's still learning, and I have to allow that to happen, and she will grow the right way. That's what children do. They are cheeky and rebellious."

Well, I could have told you that, I thought to myself. Yet maybe that was me! So I had to ask, "Who's your guide?"

"It's the gold one, it's you, it's fun. We are bouncing around the universe. It's like the planets are trampolines. I want to stay here. Hm, but still more to learn … 'eventually,' he said, but I need to learn more first. Eventually. And Stacey will be alright, but not with him [her husband]. She lives by herself with the younger two. Paige is with me. 'You just have to let go and trust.' He [Goldie] is showing me Tiana's sixteenth birthday again. 'Be there,' he says. He's funny but he's a smart-arse."

I had to admit I quite liked Goldie's sense of humour. I was intrigued that Paige would live with Judy in the future, as there were certainly no current plans for her to move. Equally intriguing was the news of creatures on other planets, though after all my reading that now didn't seem so far-fetched. Later, during our discussions, Judy revealed her thoughts about the alien creatures.

"Yeah, why not? It makes sense, and they were really cute, somewhere between a Smurf and a gremlin."

Cute, according to Judy, could mean many things. She thought her snake was cute. He, by the way, was still alive and even bigger.

There were no more regressions after that. Judy asked Goldie during one of his communications with her, and he said, "No, that's enough for now." Our hypnosis and healing sessions continued nonetheless, and the conversations between Judy and Goldie were unremitting. I remained captivated. His messages continued to range from specific to worldly, and were usually directed at Judy but sometimes to me.

◆

Four months after the "royal" regression, Judy was emotionally strong but suffering from pelvic pain and vaginal bleeding. Booked for a hysteroscopy and curettage in two days' time, some of her old anxieties had returned.

"John, someone said I might end up needing a hysterectomy. Hm … no more womb service."

She hadn't lost her sense of humour, but in view of her anxieties, a healing hypnosis was mandatory. She soon came into contact with Goldie.

"He said they'll fix it. It's fixable, just a hiccup. I'll be okay. He's going to be beside me. He knows I don't want to go. 'It's just a step in time,' he says. I told him I'm not good with hiccups." Soon after, Judy said, "He's telling me that when I took the overdose, I wasn't alone. He said, 'Why did you think you were alone? You are never alone.' He says it's not punishment. It's not my fault. He's showing me that little girl. 'How can you blame that little girl?' he says. I chose this ... this life. Maybe I didn't know it was going to be this hard, but there's good too. There's good in there. I can see the bad things happening, and then I can see the good things too. There's good and bad in every life, he says. He's saying, just trust."

Not able to help myself, I chimed in. "I suppose it's about trusting yourself as well?"

Judy laughed. "What? Are you and he on the phone? That's what he just said. It's quadraphonics, and he's going to tell me all the time, 'Let go and trust'."

As she continued to interpret Goldie's communications, she said, "I wish you could hear him because it would be so much easier! Can you hear him?"

"No," I responded, "but keep telling me what he's saying."

"He says you only get given what you can take. And I've been thinking all bad, bad, bad, and so bad comes, right? If you can think good, the scales change. And I was attracting the bad, he was saying, and that's why when you're not smiling ... if you hang with dogs you get fleas. It's a whole different outlook, and as you change that, you attract ... you attract the positive."

I had read *The Law of Attraction*, after Kate had loved it so much, but Judy certainly had not read it. Judy continued.

"And he's telling *you* to just keep doing what you are doing. It's a big world out there, but not many know this, not many. 'Keep doing what you are doing', he says, 'It's the right thing.' He says you underestimate yourself. You're still doing it. You have to believe in yourself more."

I had to admit I still had plenty of self-doubt, even though I knew this was my path. In response, I said, "I suppose some will hear it and not others?"

"But everyone will get it eventually. Everyone. Some people, on their deathbed, they change. They see it. It's only a short travel to the next realm, and it's all crying people left behind, but we are laughing up here." Judy continued. "He says love is very important, especially loving yourself. He wanted me to say that. He's telling me to keep the green healing light on my pelvis and on my back."

Directing green light to injured parts of her body from crystals was one of the techniques I had used with Judy during hypnosis.

"He says, look at your back, for instance, it's a lot better than it was, and I didn't believe it could be this much better. So he says that you just have to know it's going to get better ... think like that. Let go and trust. When I was Mum, I never did. Always waiting for bad to happen. He's saying that's not me. I died angry ... when Mum died, I'm saying 'Mum,' but that was me, you know what I mean. She was angry, angry at her life, not at me."

A smile crept over Judy's face.

"I'm happy about me. I'll love myself one day, that's for sure. Everything takes time. He says to me, you couldn't have done all this straight away. Nah, it would be worse than double shock treatment. Too much happening too quickly."

Whistling in exclamation, she continued,

"It's a process. You can't do it that quickly. It would be a million times overload. That's why our journey has been like this. He's telling you that."

"It takes time," I echoed.

"Yes, but it does happen. And you've got angels and guides too. Everyone has. He's just telling me. There are times when you are alone and you know, you know you've got an inner strength, a stronger ... a powerful ..." Judy quite suddenly turned her head around to the left, and firmly said to Goldie, "I'm trying to say it right!" She then continued. "It's a spiritual thing that you know, that others may not be aware of, but in yourself, in your heart, you know. You know you've got help in what you do."

Even if it wasn't the perfect translation, her words were a delight.

"And you'll write a book. It's half written, he says."

While Judy had long ago concluded that I should be doing the hypnosis on everyone, she had no idea I'd been contemplating writing.

"He said it's coming on. You've done more on it. He knows. It's funny seeing it. He's showing me two books: one you've written in and one you're writing in now."

Goldie could not have been more accurate. I had filled one journal and had nearly finished a second.

At the end of the hypnosis, there were a thousand topics Judy might have raised, but her first words were, "You're shitting me. As if you doubt yourself. Do you?"

The answer was easy.

"Of course I do. Everyone has doubts, and I'm certainly no exception. I just don't show you that side of me, or not very much."

Judy must have known that, but I was very aware that it suited her to see me in a strong light. As she packed up, I reminded her, "Now don't forget when you are going in for the operation, just take yourself into the garden."

"John, I don't think I need it. I feel great, no pain."

"Goldie says the operation will be fine, so let's stick to the plan."

As usual, we had run over time and there was much to contemplate. The idea that our thoughts and feelings, our consciousness, can manifest what happens in our lives remained alluring and yet daunting. Then there were the angels and guides and the book I was yet to write. It was double shock treatment.

◆

Judy's operation went well and she was understandably relieved. In the session following her surgery, while under hypnosis, Judy was visualising the light and energy from healing crystals and applying them to areas of her body that needed relief. As she applied the light she verbalised her bliss.

"It's so peaceful, it's beautiful. And you can't get that in a box, he [Goldie] says. Sometimes he can be a smart-arse."

She paused for a moment and then announced, "He said he's got something to show me. They are operating on my body. They aren't talking bad, it's respectful. It's a lot, the stirrups and straps around my legs…" Judy later remarked how that explained the bruises on her thighs. "…a big thing down my throat, hm, they drop the bottom of the bed. It's like half the bed is gone. There's a big sheet over my knees, and he's down underneath." She paused for a moment. "It's good, though. He [Goldie] says it's going to be a bit rocky but we can do it. It'll be alright but there are still hiccups."

Laughing, Judy then said, "He's showing me Tiana's birthday again."

I was having trouble keeping up, and at times Judy's voice would drop to a whisper. I felt reassured that I could return to the recording.

During a pause, I finally got a chance to ask one question that had been on my mind. "How much of your soul is in this life as Judy? How much of your over-soul is in this life?"

"A lot of it, because it's so involved ... because this is the big one before resting."

I had to add, "You know how far you've come?"

"Ten lifetimes, he said. Ten lifetimes. He said, so have you!"

I couldn't disagree. In fact, I rarely did where Goldie was concerned. Nearing the end of the hypnosis, I was keen to have a coffee and some time to think. Just as I was starting to bring Judy back to Earth, she chimed in.

"He says to put some green oil on your sore shoulder. Just thought he'd say."

Now I needed two coffees. I'd had a sore right shoulder for about six months, since lifting one of my twin grandchildren onto my shoulders. As always, I was interested in Judy's initial response after waking.

"He can be such a smart-arse, John." Then, in a sing-song voice, "You won't get that in a box! But John, I used to have shopping bags full of drugs. Not just the prescriptions but the painkillers and laxatives. Boxes and boxes."

Judy was still on medication I was prescribing, but the load was lessening.

"And John, I can't believe what my brain comes up with. What's with the shoulder?"

I explained to Judy, and she promised to get some "green oil" from Maureen. I was equally fascinated by her accurate description of the surgical bed, not to mention the information about our souls. At the same time, I felt a little apprehensive about the "hiccups" to come. What might look like a hiccup from Goldie's higher perspective didn't always seem so easy to Judy and me. Despite that, I was learning to trust that things would work out.

It was now self-evident that Judy was enjoying life. She had no desire to die, even if she did love it when she went "home." Her relationship with Jeff was solid, though she openly declared her discontent when he was behaving badly.

"John, he had his hair dyed. It looks wrong."

"Boy, is that ever the pot calling the kettle black!" I retorted in Jeff's defence.

"No, listen to me. It's wrong. It's okay for women, but men should let things go naturally." But I can't get angry. It's hard to be angry at anything. It feels like someone else is in me."

We had plenty of time that day, so Judy had a long conversation with Goldie. I was still digesting Judy's life as her mother, so early on I asked, "Was one of your lives lived as your mother?"

"Of course, yes … I was living it."

"So you can have two lives lived together at the same time? Can you ask him?" I was nothing if not persistent, and obviously needed some confirmation.

"Even her childhood, the abuse—she was abused sexually as well—I was my mum. I died angry. I was two people. I'm Marjorie Bell and I'm Judy."

I felt like I was talking to Judy's higher self or over-soul.

"Both hard lives," I thought out loud.

"But it's to show me this today. It's all here in front of me. I can see my childhood, this one, but also seeing the past ones when it's been good. And you can't have it good all the time. That's why I've come back again as my mum, as me. It's all me. I'm them. I chose this life because I didn't know how to love and to forgive, and now all that's changed. I forgive. I love. I have compassion. But he says it's time. After this one, it's time for a rest. But there's a lot still to be done in this life."

The insights and the connection with Goldie continued. "I don't hate. I'm not hate. It only makes you sick. And fear, that's worse. That eats you up, he says." Then, directed at me, "You know because you've got a spiritual view, he says, you see it from a spiritual angle. It's not just textbooks, too many textbooks."

Sometimes, Judy applied her own expletives during translation. "We've got to get to the bigger picture. We've got to get through all the shit on top and get to our bigger self. Tablets might be a band-aid in the short term, but in the long run, what you are doing is right. That's from him … from you! ... You're a white-lighter, and we were meant to be doing this. It was meant to be. That overdose ... it wasn't ... they knew about it. Everyone knew about it except us down here."

While contemplating the idea of being a white-lighter, I asked, "We agreed to do this before we came into these lives?"

"Yes, because every time you live, you learn ... learn something. And you should know what a white-lighter is. You know what that means."

I had recently read an excellent book by a medium, Laura Lynne Jackson, called *The Light Between Us*. She described people committed to communicating knowledge of psychic and spiritual matters as "light workers." I presumed this was what Judy and Goldie meant by "white-lighter." I baulked at the idea, as I didn't see myself as having done much "light work" yet, but had to admit my destiny seemed to be moving in that direction.

◆

Once again, there was a period of calm. I continued to embrace Goldie's input, while Judy continued to embrace life. Accepted as a member of the Aboriginal community, she had been invited to give a welcome to country ceremony for a group of government health dignitaries attending a seminar.

"John, they all wanted to talk to me afterwards, and I told them about the hypnosis. Then they all started telling me they were meditating. John, you have to write the book and you have to tell people what's happened to me. No, really, it's the duck's nuts; you have to do it."

"But Judy, it's not that easy to write about patients. There's confidentiality issues. People might work out who you are."

"I don't care. No, really, look at me, look how far I've come. They need to know. And John, I bumped into James the other day. He's got grandkids too. He's loving retirement. I told him how good I was and I thanked him. I told him I was 'smelling the roses.' John, I think he teared up a bit. He's a good man—he was good to me."

"I agree, he was."

"But John, I think I'm going to be boring. The other day, talking to those health people instead of saying 'What the fuck?' I came out with 'Lo and behold'!"

Nothing about Judy that morning was boring. Despite her good humour, she still had lower pelvic pain, so onto the red chair she went, where she soon connected with Goldie.

"Stacey is moving again."

"Moving house?" I asked.

"Yeah, further away. He says it doesn't matter. I'll get to them if I have to. He said don't tell her, though. She'll tell me. I keep seeing a vortex of colour. I don't know if I should go in. I want to but I'm not sure."

I encouraged her to go to the colour.

"I was scared because of the darkness. We are there, Goldie and me. It's beautiful, swirling like in a vortex and no gravity ... floating." Judy looked blissful.

Curious as ever, I asked her, "Are there other beings?"

"Yes, all familiar."

"Do you know who they are?"

"Darryl and Cindy. It's alright bro ... he said sorry and I told him it's alright. I said I'm sorry for holding a grudge."

Darryl was one of Judy's brothers, who had died in an accident when he was quite young.

"And Cindy, she's still little. And Pop Deluca, he's a green colour, beautiful emerald green. Aunty Mary. This is a holiday. It's lovely. A lady who I don't know. I feel her. She's beautiful, pink and purply. This lady is special, he [Goldie] is telling me ... it's to you ... she's with you. Someone you know. I don't know her but she's beside you. I think your grandmother. Beautiful colours ... good juju there. Hey, this is my trip!"

Even in this wonderfully connected state, Judy could be funny.

"Now we are at the other end," she said.

"Why did Goldie show you those spirits?"

"Because they are with me, they are with us, and this is what is real. I'm not alone, and when it's hard, I'm still not alone. He's telling me because he knows I felt that. He says not to be angry. I tell him I'm not, and he says, 'Yes, you are.' It's hard to fight with someone who knows. And he's telling me I have to be stronger with people. Boy, that's a hard one. You've done harder stuff than that, he says ... that's an easy one."

I appreciated it when Goldie incorporated some sensible psychology into Judy's spiritual experiences, as there were lots of people Judy had trouble saying no to. I raised this later when she was back in her usual chair.

"So, Goldie says you need to be a bit stronger with people?"

"Yeah, I know. Samantha just comes into the house smoking and I don't say no. And I need to say no to April sometimes. And John, the Koori women, there's some real politics, it's full-on, too much sometimes."

Judy then went on to discuss the characters in the vortex, especially little Cindy, who she had so loved. I had almost forgotten about Stacey when Judy raised her.

"He said she's moving again, even further away. I can't believe it."

◆

Judy missed her next appointment. She was in hospital with an impacted bowel—severe constipation. I soon received the gruesome details over the phone.

"They thought I might have to have an operation. They tried everything. I was in for two days. Then finally, John, I gave birth to an anaconda."

At her next appointment, there was still no shortage of detail.

"Apparently there's no elastic left in the bowels. The muscles don't work anymore. We have to put the green light on it. I never told you how many laxatives I used to take—sometimes a packet a day. No, seriously, it cost a fortune."

"Judy, I've brought something for you to read. When I told Mrs Webber [Judy always referred to Kate as Mrs Webber] about your impaction, she looked it up in Louise Hay's book, and here's a copy of what it said for constipation."

Judy quietly read the probable cause of bowel and colon problems, namely "the fear of letting go of the old and no longer needed, of holding onto the past." While she was thinking, I added, "So Mrs Webber thinks that even despite how well you have been, you are still having trouble letting go. I know you are doing brilliantly, but there's still some of the old fears and anger. Even Goldie mentioned that."

"Did he? John, I can't always remember everything he says, but this is trippy shit."

"Yep, I couldn't have put it better myself."

"Tell Mrs Webber thank you. I get it. She's amazing. I've seen her colours, you know."

"Really?"

"Yeah, in the hypnosis, purple and turquoise … beautiful. I think Maureen's got that book. I need a copy."

I knew Judy wasn't much of a reader, but I still lent her a copy of *You Can Heal Your Life*, at her next visit.

"And John, Stacey's moving … to some town out of Melbourne. She says it's cheaper there."

I loved it when Goldie was right. I was still writing in the second journal. My shoulder was still sore, though it was improving even without the green oil, and now Stacey was moving. What made me a little apprehensive, though, was the thought of how he had said there was still more to do and more hiccups to come. Hopefully, the faecal impaction had been one of those hiccups.

During the hypnosis that day, we focused the green crystals and lights onto her bowel. Her conversation with Goldie included, "He's telling me the piece of paper was meant to come from Mrs Webber … because if I don't see it in black and white, I don't believe."

And later, "We are all connected. One way or another, we are all connected." And, "Mrs Webber, she works from afar." I wasn't about to disagree.

Ten minutes after Judy's appointment had finished, I got a message from my secretary to say that the green light had worked: Judy had successfully been to the toilet again!

◆

Over the next four months, Judy's life was turned on its head. She had been so well, she had made little fuss about having a gynaecological review, but during the colposcopy she had biopsies. The histology had shown VIN III (vulvar intraepithelial neoplasia—meaning the cells were abnormal and potentially precancerous), and she was now booked to have it reviewed at a more specialised hospital in Melbourne in eight weeks' time.

During Judy's next three appointments with me, Goldie continued to pass on his wisdom.

"In this lifetime for me … it's all happened for a reason, he tells me.

What's happened is not right … that it happened for a reason doesn't make it right."

"In the end, it was all meant to be. It's what I chose in this life. Forgiveness. Love. Sadness and happiness.

"He's showing me good things. Watching Stacey give birth to the kids, cutting cords. Eventually, it will all be happy. I'm not the child, I'm grown up now.

"Goldie says, look at now. Look at where you are now. So much better. Forgiving. Getting healed. Knowing I'm a soul."

While discussing the topic of white-lighters with Goldie, Judy had said to him, "I want to be a white-lighter too. I want to help people. I want to not be known as the drug addict Judy. I'm just asking him if I'll ever be like that, and he said I will, and I asked how. He tells me to mind my own business and wait. I'll learn when it happens.

"He says there will be hiccups, but he says I have to be there for the kids. It's part of the journey.

"He's telling me it's going to get rocky for a while because of *where* it is and *why* it is. [I presumed they were talking about the VIN III.] It's part of letting go. It's still hard to do that. I used to resent life. I used to hate that my parents had me. But I don't now. I feel loved. But to get here, I had to go there. 'You've finally worked it out,' he said. If you aren't experiencing, you can't learn."

After that particular interaction, I remembered one of my favourite quotes, from a book called *The Afterlife of Billy Fingers,* by Annie Kagan: "The soul loves experience and doesn't fear suffering. The soul knows it can never be injured." It reminded me of the importance of living fearlessly.

Judy continued to translate Goldie's wisdom.

"It's taken thirty years but I can smell the roses … a slow learner … no, not a slow learner, he says, just a lot to learn.

"He's telling me it's going to be yucky." Judy was exhaling loudly. "But it's going to be alright. It's going to be a lot of stuff to do quickly, but I can do it.

"Believe, he's saying. *Trust* and *believe.* You have to believe for it to work. It's not just in this room. I've got to walk with it. He's telling me it's belief—belief that I can do it outside this room. It's like carrying the rock. He's telling me … just carry the rock. Take it with me wherever I go and believe. Believe that when I walk out that door that I'm healing … and I will!"

Judy had been carrying a piece of amber with her for years. She now had it permanently in a pouch that hung from around her neck.

The smell of spring was in the air, and a lot of my patients were recovering from the winter blues. I was appreciating Judy's well-being and revelling in Goldie's insights, but what happened next was never on my radar. The call came on a weekend via my paging service. Judy was in shock. Jeff had suffered a massive stroke. She had not been with him when it happened, but she had been able to spend time with him while he was in a coma and tell him that she loved him. She was at his side when he died.

17. Normal ugly rotten angry grief

...because life's too short even if we have several of them.
                                        Michael—my patient

◆

Kate's response to Jeff's death was, "How much does one person have to go through? Surely that's enough for now?" It mirrored my own. We both understood that each life was different and provided opportunities to experience, learn, and grow, but that didn't make it easy to accept. It was, however, much easier to understand why Goldie had said it would be "yucky" and why he had been so repetitive about the hiccups to come and there being much more to do. I took some solace from Judy's last session with Goldie, where he had told her, "There will be some bumps but you're nearly there." It also made sense why she had been shown Tiana's sixteenth birthday, a positive event in the future that would hopefully sustain her. Even the message about staying above the line was reminding her of how far she'd come and that she would sustain that improvement.

Staying above that line was going to be a challenge for Judy, and there was nothing easy about her consultation four days after Jeff's death. She cried throughout. She was still largely in shock. She just couldn't believe that Jeff wasn't going to be around in the future. They had been together four and a half years, and it was easily the healthiest intimate relationship she had experienced. Her commentary throughout the session was of profound sadness, and yet it was mixed with wisdom.

"This is doing my Being in, John. Everywhere I look is Jeff. I'm missing him so much. I know I chose all of this life, but I'm detesting it. Jeff and I were the go. What do I learn? Be scared to love?"

As I started to open my mouth, she said, "No don't say rah rah rah. There's no Jeff. It's a maggot."

I thought that initial catharsis was surprisingly positive given her distress. Over the session, Judy continued to pour her heart out. There was talk of suicide and joining him, but in my heart, I knew Judy wasn't going to kill herself. In the old days, she would have tried. I continued to listen but there was little else I could do to comfort her. From time to time, I would speak my mind, perhaps to soothe myself as well as Judy.

"You know he's in a good place, don't you?"

"Yeah, yeah. No, I know, but it sucks. I just don't think I can do it."

"You are just going to be really sad for a while. I don't expect you to be anything else, but I know you'll get there."

"I didn't really trust him for a long time, and then I did. And look what happens."

"But you did love him and he loved you. You know that, don't you?"

"Yeah, I know."

"And you wouldn't want to have missed that?"

"I don't know. It's just shit. I don't know if it was worth it."

"Hopefully, in time, you'll be able to feel that it was better to have taken that risk, but in the meantime it's probably going to be shit."

Later in that session, when we were talking about her fear of loss, I perhaps prematurely spoke of the changes she had made.

"And you are stronger. You're not little Judy anymore, and not that little Aboriginal girl who was taken from her family."

"You're a fucking cunt. How do you know exactly what to say and know exactly how I feel?"

That was the most reassuring statement she made during that hour. At the end of the session, I broke one of my golden rules. I gave Judy my mobile phone number on the understanding that she could text me but not ring me. It was to provide her with an opportunity to communicate without the expectation that I would respond. Even in her wrecked state, I was confident that she would honour the agreement, and she did. We agreed to another appointment the following week. I received two texts before her next appointment.

"It's another day waking up without Jeff snoring beautifully beside me. Then I naturally check the phone, no SMS or song. No more Jeff. Fuck, bro, I love him, and yes, I know he's at peace, but I miss him so much. It's times like this I feel sick and so empty, shell-like inside. This is all a maggot. I'm sad and even angry, John. Why Jeff?

"I called dial-a-psych-nurse to ask if I'm losing my mind, and they said I'm normal. Fuck, I hope Jeff heard it. Maybe they meant—normal ugly rotten angry grief."

As she sat down at the start of her next appointment, I could still see the despondent look on her face. Her slowed movements reflected a sense of helplessness. She then removed a beanie to reveal her newly shaved head.

"John, I haven't been able to sleep, and there's no colour so I had to shave it off."

According to current vernacular, she would have been described as looking butch, but as always, Judy's presentation still revealed a certain charm or even colour.

"John, I need to do the chair," she said, turning to the red chair. "I need to know what's happening to Jeff and what to do."

I requested that we first talk about how she was coping, but after twenty minutes I acquiesced. Soon after she entered her hypnotic trance, Judy's phone went off, but she was oblivious as she applied green healing light to her bowels and pelvis and back. She was soon with Goldie.

"I can do this, he said, with you and Mrs Webber. You are more in tune than what you make out to be. He contacts you more than you know, and Mrs Webber."

One could argue that Kate had been drafted into the healing team since sharing Louise Hay's message, but I suspected that at a spiritual level, she had been part of the team for a long time.

"Jeff's not in heaven yet. We might catch him, though. He told me to tell you what I was thinking. I thought before that I would go through my life again ten times over if I could have Jeff back, but he said I don't have to go through any more hurt: that Jeff is here and that I'll be with him. It'll just take time. He's saying let's travel."

"Go with him," I encouraged, "wherever he takes you."

After only a short pause, she said, "It's Jeff. He's in the garden, a different garden. He's asleep. I asked Goldie why he's there and why he's not here."

Judy looked as if she was listening for a moment. "Okay, he's waiting, it's a transitional time for him. He's surrounded by flowers ... white ones with bells. He's peaceful. He'll be there until the funeral. I asked if he couldn't go through because he hasn't got peace in his heart, but Goldie says that he can. He'll be waiting for me. He looks beautiful. It looks like a dress, but not a dress. It's like he's sleeping. He's at peace. Goldie says he's transitioning. You don't just go from here to heaven. It's probably the first time Jeff's ever rested, Goldie says. Hm, he knows Jeff."

There was another period of silence, and then Judy said, "I'll get there soon enough, but all these birthdays to deal with first. He's at peace now, and he'll go to being at total peace."

At the end of the hypnosis, Judy looked genuinely relieved, but her sadness remained.

"So it's not a beeline from here to heaven, but John, it hurts."

"I think Goldie's showing you things to reassure you or to help, but I don't think he expects you not to feel the sadness. Like you said to me after one of your deaths, when you were in that spirit world, 'It's all beautiful up here but it's all crying down on Earth,' and I suppose that's because they know up there is real and that we are never really separated."

"And John, I had to cancel the appointment at the specialist hospital for the fairy examination. ['Fairy' was Judy's new euphemism for her genitals.] I just couldn't do it."

"Fairy" is at least better than "filth," I thought to myself. I was about to enquire about the appointment but Judy beat me to it.

"Don't worry, it's booked in another fortnight."

The fact that Judy had rebooked was another good sign. Even her texts over the next week usually had something affirming in them, even if only in a small way.

"Please make this all go away. The kids miss him. I'm crying again, and it's hurting to the pit of my being, worse than ever. Bring on the abuse! Even Dad dying—yep, this is worse. I'm not sure if this love's worth all the agony. Hope you're seeing him with the flowers. So peaceful. How much learning do I have to do as it's a bit much this!"

Judy's next appointment was after Jeff's funeral.

"The funeral was shithouse. They kept calling him Jeffrey, and he hated that. And too much religion. Fair dinkum, if I crossed myself as much as they did, I would have got RSI again."

Overall, though, it was evident that she had coped quite well and had received great support from Stacey, the grandchildren, and a number of friends. She had wrestled with having very little say in the funeral, as that had been controlled by Jeff's family. In fact, I think she was quite pleased that she had coped well.

"John, check this out." Judy was showing me a text from an old Narcotics Anonymous friend who was saying she should have asserted herself and pushed back on Jeff's family.

"What would be the point of that? They're on their journey." Then, amused but mildly alarmed, "Oh my God, I can't believe I'm saying that!"

That day, Goldie informed Judy of Jeff's future trajectory.

"He's laughing at me. He said I could do it and I said I couldn't. And Jeff's not here, either."

"Can you ask him what Jeff's doing?" I suggested.

"He's got to rest for a while, then he's on another tram, another journey. I will meet him in … not his next life but the one after. He's starting it soon, but first he needs to rest. He needs to learn patience. Good luck!" Judy laughed. "He said I can't be with him in his coming life. He's off to Amsterdam. Not to be a druggie; he's just going to be there. He'll be happy but will need to learn patience … with a family! I'm not jealous, because we'll meet up in the life after that, and I'm resting."

As Judy was talking about the future, I was contemplating the concept of time. Theoretically, I knew there was no past or future, that everything was happening at once, but I still found it hard to get past the idea that time is linear. Either way, I wasn't about to interrupt.

"He'll be female, five children." Judy whistled in exclamation. "He's not in the garden now, and I thought he would be. I asked why I'm not … it's because I know, Goldie tells me, I know what's happening."

I presumed that what Judy had been shown was for her benefit. I had also pondered the nature of our transition from the low vibration of our earthly state to the high vibration of the spirit state. Perhaps all our transitioning experiences are slightly different depending on our needs. My thoughts had not stopped Judy's flow.

"And his love and his strength will never leave me … because I'm strong now. I asked why I wasn't with him in Amsterdam and he said it's because it's not my journey. The next one is his journey. He said there are two more bumps for me, and one of them is the ladies' hospital. I asked him what the other one was, but he said get through this one first."

Judy then focused on her healing lights.

"I'm lying back and directing the light, green to the tummy and fairy. Blue to the heart. Purple to the mind. He [Goldie] is telling me this is healing it; otherwise it would be a big bump, not a smaller one. I'll cope with this, he says. I'll be making the sixteenth birthday. I can go with seeing him [Jeff] after his next life. He's got things to learn. With Jeff, I had to learn love, and I'm glad I experienced it. I'm glad I loved, and he received love from me and that was good. It's just learning. I had a few things to learn in this life. Forgiveness … that's the big one, and to learn to love."

Judy was always much more peaceful in that hypnotic state, and especially when talking to Goldie. I knew her anxieties and grief would return, but her dialogue with him helped provide me with insights and a script that I could replay to her later.

Judy was coping, and in her next session she remarked on the fact that she had not hurt herself. The message from Goldie that day was on an old theme: trust and believe. At one point in their conversation, she indicated she was still scared of being hurt and had trouble trusting. She then said, "I don't want to be that little Aboriginal girl anymore."

Somewhat impulsively, I said, "The only alternative is to avoid life altogether."

As if to reinforce the point, Goldie then said to Judy, "You tried that one." Then, in a whisper, Judy echoed his words. "Everything will be alright. Trust."

The days were getting longer now, and some of my bipolar patients were more unstable than usual, which often happened around the end of spring. Life was hectic but I still had time to contemplate the steady stream of mystical insights from Judy and Goldie, and also from other patients.

Judy went to the "ladies' hospital" for review, and they agreed with the

Dr John Webber

local gynaecologist, though they noted that the largest lesion had shrunk. She was booked to have the lesions excised in another three months. The wait would not be easy. Judy was still grieving, and then out of nowhere, Paige decided she wanted to live with her. Stacey had been unwell for some time, and Paige hated school and was refusing to attend. Judy had agreed to Paige staying but was unsure how she'd cope.

Uncharacteristically, at her next appointment Judy was waiting quietly as I sat down with my notepad and pen. As if reading my mind, she started. "John, she's only fourteen, and I have to book her into the local school. She has to go. They'll take her. They were pretty good with Dylan."

Judy kept talking as she headed over to the power outlet on the wall to recharge her phone. Her hair was a fraction longer.

"John, I didn't get any calls for two days after our last appointment. I forgot to take it off aeroplane mode. So I'll just turn it off ... but I can't, because the school might ring. And John, I've got no money. It took Centrelink a year to help me with Dylan. Do you remember?"

I did remember, and knew Judy would struggle. I hoped someone would help her wade through the welfare bureaucracy.

"Will Ian help?"

"Yeah, he's great. If only Jeff were here. The kids loved him. And Dylan's been pretty good with Paige. I told him it's only fair. But John, she's tricky. I can't always believe what she says."

During those three months, Christmas passed without fanfare. We didn't visit Goldie as often, and it took a while for me to register that he had warned Judy that Paige would be living with her. When we had time for the hypnosis, the insights from Goldie, as usual, were wise, encouraging, and patient, and for Judy genuinely sustaining.

She was often shown events from the past, reminding her of how far she had come.

"I am stronger. He's showing me Dad's death. I'm running around the corridors at the hospital, taking drugs. But with Jeff, I just hugged him.

"He [Goldie] just said ... five years back ... just imagine where I am now. I wouldn't have believed. I would have said it was mad. I would have said you were mad. It's *trust* and *believing*, he said."

Being shown images of the past reinforced her progress in ways that I couldn't. Our connectedness was part of that message.

"We are all one big family. I was just trying to work out who's my family and realised that everyone is. Everyone. He's just reminded me we are all just one big family."

Goldie also reminded Judy (and me) that we can't learn someone's lessons for them.

"With Paige, he says just care for her, keep her there now, see how it goes. Just trust. Paige will get there and it won't take as long as I did. The matriarch doesn't have to fix everybody ... just be there." Judy was laughing. "Matriarch!"

I loved it when he reminded Judy that we all have supports in ways we don't understand.

"I asked him, 'Why help me?' and he said, 'Why not?' He said it's that little bit of doubt I've still got. He always picks it. He's singing the Beatles' song, With a Little Help from My Friends. He's making the crystals heavy-duty today."

Sometimes it was good old-fashioned psychology.

"I had no choice back then. It's like pointing a finger at a baby. How can I blame that baby?"

Occasionally, there was a message for me. "He said, when you see the butterflies or dragonflies, remember he's there with you. You are doing the right thing. It's to let you know you are one of them. You have had a lot of lives to get to this one, but in each one of them your heart was always there." She was laughing now. "So you weren't perfect to start with. You were nearly, he says."

I had never told Judy my story of the butterflies.

Judy finally had the excision of her perineal lesions and coped well. The doctors were happy they had removed what they needed to, but they were concerned about the area close to her anus and possibly into her rectum. She was then booked in to have further biopsies of that region, under anaesthetic, three weeks later.

"But why there? I hate it. Why there?"

"That's where..."

"I know, I know. That's where all the bad thoughts were."

"Yep that's where the *dis*-ease was. Have a read of the last chapter of Louise Hay's book. She was sexually abused when she was younger, and guess what ... that's where her cancer developed."

"Fuck. Seriously? So it's not just me?"

"No, not just you. So, how are the wounds?" I asked, as she grimaced while moving in her chair.

"Yeah, okay, but I can still feel one of the stitches. They said it will go. I can't believe I have to do it again, this time my arse. I don't want to do it. John, I feel like a bum on legs."

The main message from Goldie that day was that Judy had more to do in this life and by having the operation it was going to take away the past. He told her, "It's like your childhood has gone on for fifty-eight years, but not anymore." He says, "After the operation, we will deal with whatever comes."

After the hypnosis, she sat gingerly back in her chair and I said, "Well, Goldie says it'll be okay, so that's what I believe."

"Yes, but John, everyone's telling me not to have it. You know, Ian and Maureen."

"Judy, I don't think you can take that risk, and Goldie is saying to do both. Do the healing, the green light, and do the biopsies. And I agree with him. You know I meditate and do my own healing, but if I get my iritis, I still put the steroid drops into my eyes. I'd love to be so connected that I don't need to, but I'm not there yet. So I do both and I reckon that's what you have to do."

Judy had no less than nine biopsies of the areas around her anus and rectum. She coped wonderfully and was ecstatic when the results came through. No further action was required apart from reviews in the future.

◆

We didn't connect with Goldie as frequently through the rest of that year, but when we did, the messages remained wise, loving, and sustaining. In the meantime, Judy continued to cope with her normal ugly rotten angry grief and with looking after Dylan, Paige, and herself. It was also apparent that we had seen the last of the hiccups for now.

◆

Twenty-seven years had passed since I first saw Judy. She was one of a few patients I had been seeing for that long. Like most of my colleagues,

I have patients who have severe or chronic illnesses that need long-term treatments: support that helps them keep their heads above water and prevents further deterioration. It's not that we lose hope, as there is always room for hope, but there comes an acceptance that with such patients, significant improvement is unlikely. Six years ago I would have placed Judy in that same category. Now she was one of the exceptions.

In the years since we started using hypnosis and past-life regression, Judy had progressively become stronger and emotionally healthier. She had stopped using heroin, stopped smoking, and come off all opiate medications. She had stopped scrubbing her vagina and burning herself. From her new perspective, suicide was no longer an option. Her prescribed medications were significantly reduced, and both she and I expected to decrease them further. Though still sad about Jeff's death, she had coped remarkably well while at the same time caring for two of her grandchildren. Given that our state of mind has the ability to manifest physically, it's not surprising that years of abuse and decades of focus on her "filth" inevitably led to disease in that area. Yet even with that, she was working on healing herself while also trusting in the medical investigation and treatment of those illnesses.

Judy's life remained a very rich tapestry, yet she was kind, generous, still very funny, and far from boring. Towards the end of the year, her hair was still shortish and mostly pink, and she and Paige were off to visit a friend in Perth. Her early Christmas card read:

> *Dear little Goldie, Mrs Webber and family*
> *Well times are Grouse and things are <u>hard</u>!*
> *Here's your fucking Christmas card!*
> *Ho fucking Ho*
> *What a journey. Thank you for showing me the Way.*
> *Sincerely Judy xo*
> *Ps. See you at the sixteenth birthday party.*

18. Let go and trust

> Your task is not to seek for love but merely to seek and
> find all the barriers within yourself that you have built
> against it.
>
> *Helen Schucman*

◆

I often wonder how different my life would have been if Sam had not told me about Monica, if Margot had not given me *Many Lives, Many Masters*, and if Kate and my family had not joyfully accompanied me on this journey. I like to see it as the journey back to knowing who we really are—discovering or perhaps more accurately remembering that we are eternal souls who are always loved and never alone. We are souls that are all wonderfully connected and part of something so expansive and extraordinary that we can't go close to defining it in human terms.

Judy's journey back has been spectacular. All her life she had despised herself and was terrified of loss. She saw all her emotional and physical pain as punishment and fate, and yet with the hypnosis and the regressions, she discovered love, forgiveness, and her true self: a soul that has lived many lives. Her recovery still took years. When negative thought is so wired into someone it needs time, or, as Goldie put it, any faster and it would have been a million times overload.

Remembering who we really are means also discovering self-love. I would argue that everything I do as a psychiatrist ultimately is aimed at helping patients to feel better about themselves and ideally find a way to genuinely love themselves. It doesn't matter if the approach is Freudian, teleological, Jungian, cognitive/behavioural or existential, life here on Earth will always throw up obstacles and the challenge is to see it all and ourselves in the best possible light, to clear out the years of earthly baggage and discover the diamond that is our essence.

Of course, it's often not that easy. I know if I'd told Judy to love herself in the early days, she would have laughed in my face. I had a patient come in one day who was struggling with anxiety and marital problems, and her first words to me were, "If you tell me to love myself today I'm going to have to smash you!" When I raised the idea with another patient, he responded by symbolically sticking his fingers down his throat. Their responses are completely understandable, because for a lot of people, if not most of us, it's about moving bit by bit in that direction. Some would suggest that such a process promotes selfishness, but I believe the happier we are with ourselves, the less likely we are to do anyone harm. From a spiritual perspective, remembering who we really are can make that path even easier. Perhaps only a few of us will come to complete self-acceptance in our current lives, but as we get closer, we start to lose our fear and find more joy and peace of mind.

Involving a spiritual perspective in treatment has been wonderfully therapeutic for some of my patients. The use of past-life regressions for others, like Judy, has been life-changing. It can extinguish phobias and provide insights into unexplained fears, but more than anything it shines a light on who we really are. Understanding that makes it easier to love ourselves and navigate the hiccups.

My own journey back has been wonderfully rewarding. I see myself and everyone, including my patients, in a new light. In the past, I was quite fearful of death, and while I'm still in no hurry to leave this life, I am curious to know what my experiences will be when I die. As Goldie had hoped, I am learning to have more faith in myself, and am less anxious and certainly less angry. I am having more fun, and I'm sure that has had a positive effect on those around me. I believe we all come from the same source, and it doesn't matter if you call it "source" or "God" or "all that is" or "the infinite" or "the one." What's more, I believe we have not just come from that source: we are still part of it, all seven billion of us, no

Dr John Webber

exceptions. I love the saying, "When I bless myself, I bless the world." Life now has a lot more ease.

I think it is likely that the next major shift in science will relate to consciousness. Excitingly, quantum theory and the exploration of consciousness are just starting to hint at the truth of our connectedness and even our capacity to influence outcomes. The enormity and complexity of why we are here and how we are here, I am sure, goes spectacularly beyond our most sophisticated explanations.

Yet we are all wonderfully individual. How boring would this world be if we were all the same? Within our differences lies the potential to learn from a multitude of different experiences. We sometimes choose particularly difficult lives because we have a desire to learn and because we know we can never truly be harmed. Goldie said that by choice we live lives with good and bad—sometimes more good, sometimes more bad. He also said that when it's bad, it doesn't make it right, but in the end it is all as it's meant to be. Even if that is true, it doesn't mean we should give in to pain and suffering. Where possible, we need to shift our attention away from the negatives.

The challenge is to quieten our minds and make every effort to move ourselves towards an attitude and a feeling that is a bit more positive, and to find a way to feel better about ourselves. Psychological therapies are starting to teach us that, and more recently, mindfulness and meditation—around since ancient times—are helping in the same way. In terms of treatments, I'm not suggesting we throw out the baby with the bathwater, as clearly we still need medications and physical treatments. For me, the additional spiritual approach, when it fits, adds an exciting new dimension.

It remains extraordinary to me that we choose to squeeze into these bodies and experience our human lives with all their joy and pain, not just once but many times. It makes sense that at the same time, we elect to forget our higher origins and explore all that this Earth has to offer. Until we have left this world, we will probably never completely understand it all.

During the exciting time when both Kate and I were exploring all the new information about past lives, near-death experiences, mediums, and other psychic phenomena and their associated wisdoms, Kate had a dream. In the dream, she saw herself in a play.

"It was like *The Pirates of Penzance*," she said. "I had my role and you were playing the role of the Pirate King. After the play, we were all chatting about how it went for each of us."

Kate then explained that she knew it was a metaphor for life, that this is the play and we've all chosen a role. It's a chance to experience something new, but it's not who we really are. And so, if there is one thing you take away from reading this book, it would be to remember that *this* is not who you really are. Your current character is but a role you have chosen. It may be simple, it may be complex, it may be easy or hard. Either way, try to have some fun. Try to enjoy it as best you can, but remember it's not who you really are. Who you really are is love and joy and peace and so much more.

Judy finally took down the sign that said, "Good morning, let the stress begin" from her bedroom wall. She was miraculously able to forgive those who had abused her, and even more importantly, she was able to forgive herself. Like more and more people, she touched on some understanding of the choices our souls have made and the joy one feels in that spirit state, and as Goldie would say, she's learned to "let go and trust."

Acknowledgements

My heartfelt thanks go to many people.

Kate—you are the love of my life and no doubt many other lives. This book would not have happened without you. Goldie and Judy know that. Your vital feedback, infectious passion, patience, typing, editing, and organisational skills, and above all your love, sustained me.

Margot, Tom, Jess, Harry, Sam, and Sally—thank you all for your amazing support. Margot, Tom and Jess, you all got me over the line. Your enthusiasm, insightful comments, and creativity are deeply appreciated— to say nothing of Margot giving me *Many Lives, Many Masters* in the first place.

Richard and Ali—you have been great collaborators throughout the journey and continue to be.

Jenny—your courage led to the expansion of my world.

Ben Hourigan—As an editor, you described yourself as a 'stickler', and that worked beautifully for me. I'm appreciative of the time and meticulous expertise that you have shared with me while working on *The Red Chair*.

Patients and friends whose stories are contained in this book—in different ways, you have all contributed to the wonderful changes in me and hopefully to others in the future.

Many other patients have taught me through their regressions, perspectives, and enthusiasm. They will know who they are and I am truly grateful.

Quote Sources

"Progress is impossible without change, and those who cannot change their minds cannot change anything."

George Bernard Shaw
Everyone's Political What's What (1944)

♦

"It is almost an absurd prejudice to suppose that existence can only be physical. As a matter of fact, the only form of existence of which we have immediate knowledge is psychic. We might well say, on the contrary, that physical existence is a mere inference, since we know of matter only in so far as we perceive psychic images mediated by the senses."

Carl Jung
The Collected Works of C.G. Jung Volume 11.Psychology and Religion: West and East

♦

"My religiosity consists of a humble admiration of the infinitely superior spirit that reveals itself in the little we can comprehend about the knowable world. That deeply emotional conviction of the presence of a superior reasoning power, which is revealed in the incomprehensible universe, forms my idea of God."

Albert Einstein

Permission granted, The Hebrew University of Jerusalem, archival number: AEA 48-380

"Forgiveness is for yourself because it frees you. It lets you out of that prison you put yourself in."

Louise Hay

Louise L. Hay Quotes. BrainyQuote.com, BrainyMedia Inc, 2019. https://www.brainyquote.com/quotes/louise_ l_hay_598087, accessed October 28, 2019.

◆

"For us believing physicists, the distinction between past, present, and future is only a stubbornly persistent illusion."

Albert Einstein

Permission granted, The Hebrew University of Jerusalem, archival number: AEA 7-245

◆

"You are not a single "you."
No, you are the sky and the deep sea.
Your mighty "Thou," which is nine hundredfold,
is the ocean, the drowning place
of a hundred "thous" within you."

Jelaluddin Rumi

The Rumi Collection, ed. Kabir Helminski (Boston:Shambhala, 1998), 81.

◆

"The first problem for all of us, men and women, is not to learn but to unlearn."

Gloria Steinem

"'Women's Liberation' Aims to Free Men, Too." *Washington Post*, 7 June 1970, 192.

◆

"The soul loves experience and doesn't fear suffering. The soul knows it can never be injured."

Annie Kagan
The Afterlife of Billy Fingers

◆

"Your task is not to seek for love but merely to seek and find all the barriers within yourself that you have built against it."

Helen Schucman
A Course in Miracles, (T-16.IV.7:1), copyright 2007 by the Foundation for Inner Peace, 448 Ignacio Blvd.,#306, Novato, CA 94949, www.acim.org and info@acimstaging.wpengine.com, used with permission.

About the author

Raised and educated in Melbourne, Australia, Dr John Webber, MBBS, DPM, FRANZCP completed his medical degree at Melbourne University and his intern years at the Royal Melbourne Hospital. Initially drawn to a surgical path, he was eventually drawn by his heart and life circumstances to a career in psychiatry. His first years of psychiatric training were at the Royal Melbourne Hospital psychiatry department, and his training later included a year at the Melbourne Neuropsychiatry Centre.

Dr Webber completed his specialist qualification through the Royal Australia and New Zealand College of Psychiatrists, and has since worked in a successful private practice for thirty years. His areas of interest include bipolar disorder, depressive disorders, and anxiety disorders. Eight years ago, events that included reading *Many Lives, Many Masters*, by Brian Weiss, inspired him to include hypnosis, past-life regression, and a greater appreciation of psychic and spiritual matter in his practice.